THE ARTICLES

OF THE

SYNOD OF DORT.

TRANSLATED FROM THE LATIN, WITH NOTES,

BY THE

REV. THOMAS SCOTT, D. D.

WITH AN

INTRODUCTORY ESSAY.

BY THE

REV. SAMUEL MILLER, D. D.
Late Professor in the Theological Seminary, Princeton, N. J.

PHILADELPHIA:
PRESBYTERIAN BOARD OF PUBLICATION.
No. 265 Chestnut Street.

Stereotyped by JESPER HARDING,
NO. 57 SOUTH THIRD ST., PHILADELPHIA.

CONTENTS.

INTRODUCTORY ESSAY.

BY THE REV. SAMUEL MILLER, D. D.

THE convocation and proceedings of the Synod of Dort may be considered as among the most interesting events of the seventeenth century. The Westminster Assembly of divines was, indeed, more immediately interesting to British and American Presbyterians; and the works of that celebrated Assembly, as monuments of judgment, taste, and sound theology, have certainly never been equalled by those of any other uninspired ecclesiastical body that ever convened. Yet the Synod of Dort had, undoubtedly, a species of importance peculiar to itself, and altogether pre-eminent. It was not merely a meeting of the select divines of a single nation, but a convention of the Calvinistic world, to bear testimony against a rising and obtrusive error; to settle a question in which all the Reformed Churches of Europe had an immediate and deep interest. The question was, whether the opinions of Arminius, which were then agitating so many minds, could be reconciled with the Confession of the Belgic Churches.

The opinions denominated Arminian had been substantially taught long before Arminius appeared. The doctrine of Cassian of Marseilles, in the fifth century, commonly styled Semi-Pelagianism, was almost exactly the same system. Bolsec, too, in Geneva, about the year

1552, according to some, had taught very much the same doctrine, though justly regarded as infamous on account of his shameful moral delinquencies. And about fifteen or twenty years before Arminius arose, Corvinus, in Holland, had appeared as the advocate of opinions of similar import. But having less talent than Arminius, and being less countenanced by eminent men, his error made little noise, and was suffered quietly to sink into insignificance, until a stronger and more popular man arose to give it new consequence, and a new impulse.

James Arminius, or Harmensen, was born at Oudwater, in south Holland, in the year 1560. His father died when he was an infant; and he was indebted to the charity of several benevolent individuals for the whole of his education. At one time he was employed as a servant at a public inn,* and in this situation was so much noticed for his activity, intelligence, wit, and obliging deportment, that numbers became interested in his being enabled to pursue the cultivation of his mind. Accordingly, by one of his patrons, he was placed, for a time, in the University of Utrecht; on his decease, by another, in the University of Marpurg, in Hesse; and finally, by a third, in that of Leyden. In 1582, in the twenty-second year of his age, the magistrates of Amsterdam had received such impressions of his promising talents, and of his diligent application to study, that they sent him, at the public expense, to Geneva, which was then considered as the great centre of theological instruction for the Reformed Churches. In that far-famed institution Theodore Beza then presided, with equal honour to himself, and accept-

* Life of Wallæus, one of the members of the Synod of Dort.

ance to the students. Here Arminius, as before, manifested much intellectual activity and ardour of inquiry; but indulging a spirit of self-sufficiency and insubordination, in opposing some of the philosophical opinions held and taught by the leading professors at Geneva, and delivering private lectures to turn away the minds of the students from the instructions of their teachers, he became a kind of malcontent, and was constrained to withdraw from that institution. This circumstance somewhat impaired that confidence in his prudence which his patrons had before reposed. Still they were willing to overlook it. After travelling eight or ten months in Italy, he returned for a short time to Geneva, and soon afterwards to Holland, where he met with no small acceptance in his profession. Such was his popularity, that, in 1588, he was elected one of the ministers of Amsterdam, and entered on a pastoral charge in that city, with every prospect of honour, comfort, and usefulness. But his restless, innovating spirit soon began, in his new situation, again to disclose itself. Not long after his settlement, the doctrine of Beza concerning Predestination was publicly opposed by some ministers of Delft, in a tract which they printed on this subject. When this publication appeared, Martin Lydius, professor of Divinity at Franequar, having a high opinion of the learning and talents of Arminius, judged him to be the most proper person he was acquainted with to answer it; and, accordingly, urged him to undertake the task. Arminius, in compliance with this request from his venerable friend, undertook to refute the heretical work; but during the examination of it, and while balancing the reasoning on both sides, he went over to the opinion which he had been employed to refute; and even carried it further than the ministers of Delft had done. This change of opinion, which took place about the year 1591, and which he was not long in causing to be understood, soon excited public attention. About the same time, in a course of public lectures, delivered in his own pulpit, on the Epistle to the Romans, he still further disclosed his erroneous views. He was soon accused of departing from the Belgic Confession, and many of his brethren began to look upon him and his opinions with deep apprehension. Such, however, were the vigilance and firmness manifiested by the other members of his Classis, that they so far curbed and counteracted him as to prevent the agitation of the controversy, which it seems to have been his intention to excite.

Arminius, however, though deterred, at that early period, from public and open controversy, exerted himself in a more private way, with considerable effect. With some divines, whose friendship he had before conciliated, his talents, his learning, his smooth address, and his insinuating eloquence were successful in winning them to his opinions. The celebrated Uytenbogart and Borrius were among the number of his early converts and followers. He also took unwearied pains to gain over to his opinions some of the leading laymen of the country, and soon enlisted several of them in his cause.

In the year 1602, when the illustrious Francis Junius, an eminent Reformer, and no less eminent as a Professor of Divinity in the University of Leyden, was removed by death, to the great grief of the Belgic churches, Uytenbogart, who was just mentioned as a particular friend and partisan of Arminius, proposed, and, with great zeal, recommended him to the Curators of the University, as a candidate for the vacant Professorship. The leading Belgic ministers, hearing of this recommendation, and deeply apprehensive of the consequences of electing such a man to so important a station, besought both Uytenbogart and the Curators of the University to desist from all attempts to place in such an office one who was the object of so much suspicion. But these entreaties were disregarded. The recommendation of him was prosecuted with undiminished zeal, and the Curators at length elected and formally called him to the vacant chair.

The call being laid, as usual, before the Classis of Amsterdam, that body declined to put it into his hands. They supposed that he was more likely to prove mischievous in the office to which he was called than in his pastoral charge, where he was more immediately under the supervision and restraint of his brethren in the ministry. But, at length, at the repeated and earnest entreaties of Uytenbogart, of the Curators, and of Arminius himself, he was permitted to accept the call, and was regularly dismissed from the Classis to enter on his new office. This dismission, however, was granted upon the express condition, that he should hold a conference with Gomarus, one of the theological Professors in the same University with that to which he was called; and should remove from himself all suspicion of heterodoxy, by a full and candid declaration of his opinions in regard to the leading doctrines of the Gospel; and, moreover, the Classis exacted from him a solemn promise, that if it should be found that he held any opinions different from the Belgic Confession, he would refrain from disseminating them. This conference was held in the presence of the Curators of the University, and the Deputies of the Synod, in the course of which Arminius solemnly disavowed Pelagian opinions; declared his full belief in all that Augustine had written against those opinions; and promised in the most explicit manner that he would teach nothing contrary to the received doctrines of the Church. Upon these declarations and promises he was placed in the Professorship.

On first entering upon his Professorship he seemed to take much pains to remove from himself all suspicion of heterodoxy, by publicly maintaining theses in favour of the received doctrines;—doctrines which he afterwards zealously contradicted. And that he did this contrary to to his own conviction at the time, was made abundantly evident afterwards by some of his own zealous friends. But after he had been in his new office a year or two, it was discovered that it was his constant practice to deliver one set of opinions in his professorial chair, and a very different set by means of private confidential manuscripts circulated among his pupils.* He was also accustomed, while he publicly recommended the characters and opinions of the most illustrious Reformed divines, artfully to insinuate such things as were adapted, indirectly, to bring them into discredit, and to weaken the arguments usually brought for their support. He also frequently intimated to his pupils, that he had many objections to the doctrines usually deemed orthodox, which he intended to make known at a suitable time. It was observed, too, that some pastors who were known to be on terms of great in-

* This fact, so dishonourable to the integrity of Arminius, is so well attested by various Dutch writers of undoubted credit, that it cannot be reasonably called in question.

timacy with him, were often giving intimations in private that they had adopted the new opinions, and not a few of his pupils began to manifest symptoms of being infected with the same errors.

The churches of Holland observing these and other things of a similar kind, became deeply apprehensive of the consequences; they, therefore, enjoined upon the Deputies, to whom the supervision of the church was more especially committed, to inquire into the matter, and to take the earliest and most decisive measures to prevent the apprehended evil from taking deeper root. In consequence of this injunction, the Deputies of the churches of North and South Holland waited on Arminius, informed him of what they had heard, and urged him, in a friendly manner, if he had doubts or difficulties respecting any of the received doctrines of the Belgic churches, either to make known his mind in a frank and candid manner to his brethren in private; or to refer the whole affair, officially, to the consideration and decision of a Synod.

To this address of the Deputies, Arminius replied, that he had never given any just cause for the reports of which they had heard; but that he did not think proper to enter into any conference with them, as the Deputies of the churches; that if, however, they chose as private ministers, to enter into a conversation with him on the points in question, he was ready to comply with their wishes; *provided* they would engage, on their part, that if they found any thing erroneous in his opinions, they would not divulge it to the Synod which they represented. The Deputies considering this proposal as unfair, as unworthy a man of integrity, and as likely to lead to no useful result, very properly declined accepting it, and retired without doing anything further.

In this posture of affairs, several of the magistrates of Leyden urged Arminius to hold a conference with his colleagues in the University, before the Classis, respecting those doctrines to which he had objections, that the extent of his objections might be known. But this he declined. In the same manner he treated one proposal after another, for private explanation; for calling a national Synod to consider the matter; or for any method whatever of bringing the affair to a regular ecclesiastical decision. Now a Classis, then a Synod, and at other times secular men attempted to move in the case; but Arminius was never ready, and always had insurmountable objections to every method proposed for explanation or adjustment. It was evident that he wished to gain time; to put off any decisive action in the case, until he should have such an opportunity of influencing the minds of the leading secular men of the country as eventually to prepare them to take side with himself. Thus he went on evading, postponing, concealing, shrinking from every inquiry, and endeavouring secretly to throw every possible degree of odium on the orthodox doctrines, hoping that, by suitable management, their advocates both in the church and among the civil rulers might be gradually diminished, so as to give him a good chance of a majority in any Synod which might be eventually called.

This is a painful narrative. It betrays a want of candour and integrity on the part of a man otherwise respectable, which it affords no gratification even to an adversary to record. It may be truly said, however, to be the stereotyped history of the commencement of every heresy which has arisen in the Christian church. When heresy rises in an evangelical body, it is never frank and open. It always begins by skulking, and assuming a disguise. Its advocates, when together, boast of great improvements, and congratulate one another on having gone greatly beyond the "old dead orthodoxy," and on having left behind many of its antiquated errors: but when taxed with deviations from the received faith, they complain of the unreasonableness of their accusers, as they "differ from it *only in words.*" This has been the standing course of errorists ever since the apostolic age. They are almost never honest and candid as a party, until they gain strength enough to be sure of some degree of popularity. Thus it was with Arius in the fourth century, with Pelagius in the fifth, with Arminius and his companions in the seventeenth, with Amyraut and his associates in France soon afterwards, and with the Unitarians in Massachusetts, toward the close of the eighteenth and the beginning of the nineteenth centuries. They denied their real tenets, evaded examination or inquiry, declaimed against their accusers as merciless bigots and heresy-hunters, and strove as long as they conld to appear to agree with the most orthodox of their neighbors; until the time came when, partly from inability any longer to cover up their sentiments, and partly because they felt strong enough to come out, they at length avowed their real opinions. Arminius, in regard to talents, to learning, to eloquence, and to general exemplariness of moral deportment, is undoubtedly worthy of high praise: but if there be truth in history, his character as to integrity, candour, and fidelity to his official pledges and professions, is covered with stains which can never by any ingenuity be effaced.

At length, after various attempts to bring Arminius to an avowal of his real opinions had failed, he was summoned by the States General, in 1609, to a conference at the Hague. He went, attended by several of his friends, and met Gomarus, accompanied with a corresponding number of orthodox divines. Here again the sinister designs and artful management of Arminius and his companions were manifested, but overruled; and he was constrained, to a considerable extent, to explain and defend himself. But before this conference was terminated, the agitation of his mind seems to have preyed upon his bodily health. He was first taken apparently in a small degree unwell, and excused himself for a few days to the States General; but at length grew worse, was greatly agitated in mind, and expired on the 19th day of October, 1609, in the forty-ninth year of his age. His mind, in his last illness, seems to have been by no means composed. "He was sometimes heard," says Bertius, his warm friend and panegyrist—"He was sometimes heard, in the course of his last illness, to groan and sigh, and to cry out, 'Woe is me, my mother, that thou hast borne me a man of strife, and a man of contention to the whole earth. I have lent to no man on usury, nor have men lent to me on usury; yet every one doth curse me!'"

Attempts have been made to show that Arminius did, in fact, differ very little from the reeeived doctrines of the Belgic churches; nay, that he, on the whole, coincided with sublapsarian Calvinists; and of course, was most unjustly accused of embracing the heresy since called by his name. It is evident that Dr. Mosheim, himself an Arminian, was not of this opinion. He plainly thought, that the friends of the Belgic Confession had much more reason to apprehend hostility on the part of Arminius and his followers, to the essential principles of their creed, than their published language would seem to intimate. And the Rev. Dr. Murdock, the latest and best translator of Mosheim, has delivered the following opinion, which will probably commend itself to the judgment of all well informed and impartial readers.

"It is a common opinion that the early Arminians, who flourished before the Synod of Dort, were much purer and more sound than the later ones, who lived and taught after that council; and that Arminius himself only rejected Calvin's doctrine of absolute decrees, and its necessary consequences, while, in everything else, he agreed with the Reformer; but that his disciples, and especially Episcopius, boldly passed the limits which their master had wisely established, and went over to the camp of the Pelagians and Socinians. But it appears to me very clear, that Arminius himself revolved in his own mind, and taught to his disciples, that form of religion which his followers afterwards professed; and that the latter, especially Episcopius, only perfected what their master taught them, and casting off fear, explained it more clearly. I have as a witness, besides others of less authority, Arminius himself, who, in his will, drawn up a little before his death, explicitly declares that his aim was to bring all sects of Christians, with the exception of the Papists, into one community and brotherhood. The opinion that Arminius himself was very nearly orthodox, and not an Arminian, in the common acceptation of the term, has been recently advocated by Professor Stuart, of Andover, in an article expressly on the Creed of Arminius, in the Biblical Repository, No. II., Andover, 1831, see pp. 293

and 301. To such a conclusion the learned Professor is led principally, by an artful and imposing statement made by Arminius to the magistrates of Holland, in the year 1608, one year before his death, on which Mr. Stuart puts the most favourable construction the words will bear. But from a careful comparison of this declaration of Arminius, with the original five articles of the Arminian creed, (which were drawn up almost in the very words of Arminius, so early as the year 1610, and exhibited by the Remonstrants in the conference at the Hague, in 1611; and were afterwards, together with a full explanation and vindication of each article, laid before the Synod of Dort, in 1617, changing, however, the dubitation of the fifth article into a positive denial of the saints perseverance,) it will, I think, appear manifest, that Arminius himself actually differed from the orthodox of that day, on all the five points; and that he agreed substantially with the Remonstrants on all those doctrines for which they were condemned in the Synod of Dort. And that such was the fact, appears to have been assumed without hesitation by the principal writers of that and the following age, both Remonstrants and Contra-remonstrants."*

It was fondly hoped by many that when Arminius died, the controversy to which his speculations had given rise, would have died and been buried with him. But this, unhappily, by no means, proved to be the case. It soon appeared that a number of Belgic divines of no small name had embraced his sentiments, and could by no means be persuaded to desist from propagating them; and in 1610 they were organized into a body, or formal

* Murdock's Mosheim, III., 508, 509.

confederacy; and in this capacity presented to the States General an address, which they styled a Remonstrance, from which the whole party afterwards obtained the name of Remonstrants. The particular object of this paper was to solicit the favour of the government, and to secure protection against the ecclesiastical censures to which they felt themselves exposed. This step amounted to a kind of schism, and greatly distressed the Belgic churches. Another event soon occurred which excited deeper and still more painful apprehension among the friends of orthodoxy. When the Curators of the University came to fill the professorial chair which had been rendered vacant by the death of Arminius, the Deputies of the churches earnestly besought them to select a man free from all suspicion of heterodoxy, as one of the best means of restoring peace to the University and the church. But to no purpose. The Remonstrants had, by some means, so prepossessed the minds of the Curators, that Conrad Vorstius, a minister and professor at Steinfurt, in Germany, a man suspected of something much worse than even Arminianism, was selected to fill the office, and Uytenbogart, one of the most able and zealous of the Arminian party, was appointed to go to Steinfurt, to solicit his dismission and removal to Leyden. The orthodox ministers and churches protested against this choice. They compared it to "driving a nail into an inflamed and painful ulcer;" and earnestly besought the States General not to permit a step so directly calculated still further to disturb and corrupt the churches. Vorstius had, a short time before, published a book "*De Natura et Attributis Dei*," and had also edited, with some alterations, a book published by Socinus the younger, on the Scriptures, from both which it appeared that he leaned to Socinian opinions. Notwithstanding this, however, the Remonstrants were bent on his election, and it was with the utmost difficulty that their plan for placing him in the vacant chair was defeated. In short, their conduct in the case of Vorstius alone, was quite sufficient to show, that the apprehensions of the orthodox concerning the corrupt character of their opinions, were by no means excessive or unjust. James I. king of England, having read the book of Vorstius, a book concerning the nature and attributes of God, and conceiving it to be replete with radical error, addressed a letter to the States General, exhorting them "not to admit such a man into the important office of teacher of theology; and, further, commanded his ambassador at the Hague, to use his utmost influence to prevent the introduction into such a Professorship, of a man, as he expressed it—rendered infamous by so many and great errors, and who ought to be banished from their territories, rather than loaded with public honours." "In short," said the king, "since God has been pleased to dignify me with the title of 'Defender of the Faith,' if Vorstius is kept any longer, we shall be obliged not only to separate from those heretical churches, but also to consult all the other Reformed churches, in order to know which is the best way of extirpating and sending back to hell those cursed heresies which have recently sprung up; we shall be forced to forbid the young people of our kingdom to frequent such an infected University as that of Leyden." By these and various other sources of influence, the Remonstrants were scarcely prevented from putting Vorstius into the vacant Professorship. Still, though disappointed, they were not disheartened, or diminished in number. On the contrary, the election, soon afterwards, of Episcopius, a leading man of their party, to a Professorship in the University of Leyden, seemed to give them new strength and new hopes. It became also more and more evident that some men of no small influence in the civil government of the country, had become friendly to the Remonstrants, and strongly disposed to pursue a course which should secure at least impunity to them as a party. Hence the repeated manifestation of unwillingness on the part of the States General to promote the convening of a National Synod, or the adoption of any other plan for bringing the Remonstrants to discipline. It was evidently the favourable object of the Remonstrants and their friends, both in church and state, to do nothing; to secure the toleration of the growing errors, and to allow the Remonstrants as good a standing as the orthodox in the national church. Accordingly, when anxious efforts were made, in 1611, and again in 1613, to bring the affairs of the church to an adjustment and pacification, the friends of truth were baffled and disappointed. Every effort to bring on a crisis, or, in any form, to call the Remonstrants to an account, was resisted and evaded; and the state of things was, every day, becoming more distressing and alarming. Confusion, and even persecution ensued. Some of the orthodox pastors were suspended, and others driven from their charges, because they could not conscientiously receive those who avowed Arminian opinions into the communion of the church.

In this situation of things, when the very pillars of society seemed to be shaken; when the ruling powers of the State were seen to be more and more favourable to the erroneous party; and when everything portended the approach of a tremendous crisis—it pleased God to employ an instrument for promoting the advancement of his cause who by no means loved that cause, and who yet was placed in circumstances which at once prompted and enabled him to favour it. James I., king of England, a man of very small mind, and of still less moral or religious principle, having been born and bred in a Calvinistic community, and coming to the throne of England when the leading clergy of that part of his dominions, as well as of the North, were almost unanimously Calvinistic, fell in with the fashionable creed, and was disposed, as his manner was, in every thing, officiously to exert his royal power in its favour. He, therefore, in the year 1617, addressed a friendly, but admonitory letter to the States General, in which he earnestly recommended the calling a national synod, to vindicate the genuine doctrines of the Reformation, and to restore tranquillity to the agitated Belgic churches. About the same time, Maurice, the prince of Orange, and the Head of the United Provinces, took the same ground, and urged the same thing. When the Arminian party perceived that the popular current was beginning to run in this direction, and that there was some prospect of a national synod being called, they were filled with uneasiness, and strove by all the means in their power to prevent it. But their evasive and intriguing arts were now in vain: and although they began to manifest a spirit more like revolt and sedition than before, yet now the state of the public mind was such, that their violence only served to show the greater necessity of some efficient measure for meeting and subduing their turbulence.

At length a decree was issued by the States General in 1618, ordering that a National Synod should convene in the following November, at Dort, a considerable city of South Holland. The method prescribed for the convocation of this Synod, was, that a provincial Synod should meet in each of the provinces, from which six persons should be delegated to attend the General Synod. And, in most cases, the plan adopted was to appoint four ministers, and two ruling elders from each of the provincial synods, together with at least one professor from each of the universities.

It had been originally intended that this Synod should be formed of delegates from the Belgic churches only; but at the pointed request of James I., king of England, seconded, at his suggestion, by Maurice, prince of Orange, it was determined to invite eminent divines from foreign churches to sit and vote in the Synod. Accordingly letters were addressed to the king of Great Britain; to the deputies of the Reformed Churches of France; to the Electors of the Palatinate and Brandenburgh; to the Landgrave of Hesse; to the four Protestant Cantons of Switzerland, viz. Zurich, Berne, Basle, and Schaffhausen; and to the Republics of Geneva, Bremen, and Embden, whom they entreated to delegate some of their most pious, learned, and prudent theologians, who, in conjunction with the deputies of the Belgic churches, should labour to compose the differences, and decide the controversies which had arisen in those churches.

The Reformed churches of France, in compliance with the requests made to them, appointed Andrew Rivet and Peter du Moulin, as their delegates to attend this Synod; but just as they were about to set out for Dort, in pursuance of their appointment, the king of France issued an edict, forbidding their attendance. In consequence of this interdict, the churches of France were not represented in the Synod.

It would be wrong to omit stating, that before the Synod came together, a day of solemn prayer and fasting was appointed, to deprecate the wrath of God and to implore his gracious presence and blessing on the approaching Assembly. This day was appointed by the States General, and observed with great solemnity.

The Synod convened, agreeably to the call of the States General, in the city of Dort, on the 13th day of November, A. D. 1618. It consisted of thirty nine Pastors, and eighteen Ruling Elders delegated from the Belgic churches, together with five Professors from the Universities of Holland; and also of Delegates from all the foreign Reformed churches which had been invited to send them, excepting those of France before spoken of. The delegates from the foreign Reformed churches on the Continent, all of whom were Presbyterian, were nineteen. The delegates from Great Britain were five, viz: George Carleton, Bishop of Llandaff; Joseph Hall, Dean of Worcester, and afterwards Bishop, successively, of Exeter and Norwich; John Davenant, Professor of Divinity in the University of Cambridge, and afterwards Bishop of Salisbury; Samuel Ward, Archdeacon of Taunton, and Theological Professor in the University of Cambridge; and Walter Balcanequal, of Scotland, representing the Established Church of North Britain.

The Synod thus constituted, consisted, in all, of eighty-six members. No Arminians, it would appear, were elected members of the Synod, excepting three from the Province of Utrecht; and of these only one was admitted to a seat.

It is perfectly evident from the foregoing statement, that the leading divines, and the governing policy of the Church of England, at the date of this Synod, were very far from sanctioning the spirit which has since risen in that establishment, and which has manifested itself, for a number of years past, among many of that denomination of Christians in the United States. Here we see a prelatical bishop and three other dignitaries of the Church of England, two of whom were afterwards bishops, sitting in a solemn ecclesiastical body, and for months together deliberating, praying, and preaching with an assembly, all of whom but themselves were Presbyterians. This was a practical recognition, of the strongest kind, of the Presbyterian Church as a true Church of Christ; and demonstrated that the great and learned and good men who directed the councils of the Church of England at that time, never thought of denying, either in word or act, her just claim to this character. Some high-church men, indeed, of modern times, either ignorant of facts, or so prejudiced as to be totally blind to the lights of history, have alleged that the States General pointedly requested the king of England to send delegates to this Synod; and that he, unwilling to reject their solicitation, was over persuaded to depart, on one occasion, from the principles which ordinarily governed him and his Church. This statement is altogether incorrect. The solicitation was all the other way. The king of England, though he had nothing, strictly speaking, to do with the business, seemed fond of meddling with it; interposed from time to time in a way in which no other than a weak, officious, pedantic, and arrogant man would have thought of doing; and pressed the States General to adopt a plan which would open the way for the admission of delegates from his Church to the Synod.

And to his wishes and policy in this matter his leading divines acceded. It would have been difficult to select men of more respectable character for talents, learning, piety, and ecclesiastical influence, than those who were nominated and commissioned to take their seats in that Synod. They deliberated for months with Presbyterians; preached in Presbyterian pulpits; united in Presbyterian devotions; recognized Presbyterian churches as sister churches, and their ministers as brethren in office and in hope. O how different the language of many prelatists of later times—many of them, it must be confessed, indeed, pigmies in talents, learning, and piety, when compared with the giants who acted their parts on the occasion of which we speak!

When Bishop Hall took leave of the Synod, from which he was obliged to retire on account of ill health, he declared, "There was no place upon earth so like heaven as the Synod of Dort, and where he should be more willing to dwell;" (Brandt's History, Session 62,) and the following extract from a sermon which he delivered in Latin, before that venerable Synod, contains a direct and unequivocal acknowledgment of the Church of Holland as a true Church of Christ. It was delivered November 29, 1618, and founded on Eccles. vii. 16:

"His serene majesty, our king James, in his excellent letter, admonishes the States General, and in his instructions to us hath expressly commanded us to urge this with our whole might, to inculcate this one thing, that you all continue to adhere to the common faith, and the Confession of your own and the other churches; which if you do, O happy Holland! O chaste Spouse of Christ! O prosperous republic! this, your afflicted church, tossed with the billows of differing opinions, will yet reach the harbour, and safely smile at all the storms excited by her cruel adversaries. That this may at length be obtained, let us seek for the things which make for peace. We are brethren; let us also be colleagues! What have we to do with the infamous titles of party names? We are Christians; let us also be of the same mind. We are one body; let us also be unanimous. By the tremendous name of the Omnipotent God; by the pious and loving bosom of our common mother; by our own souls; by the holy bowels of Jesus Christ, our Saviour, my brethren, seek peace, pursue peace." (See the whole in the Acta Synodi Nat. Dord. 38.)

But this excellent prelate went further. A little more than twenty years after his mission to Holland, and when he had been made Bishop of Exeter, and advanced to the diocese of Norwich, he published his Irenicum, (or Peacemaker,) in which we find the following passage:— "Blessed be God, there is no difference, in any essential point, between the Church of England and her sister Reformed Churches. We unite in every article of Christian doctrine, without the least variation, as the full and absolute agreement between their public Confessions and ours testifies. The only difference between us consists in our mode of constituting the external ministry; and even with respect to this point we are of one mind, because we all profess to believe that it is not an essential of the Church, (although in the opinion of many it is a matter of importance to her well-being,) and we all retain a respectful and friendly opinion of each other, not seeing any reason why so small a disagreement should so produce any alienation of affection among us." And after proposing some common principles, on which they might draw more closely together, he adds—"But if a difference of opinion, with regard to these points of external order, *must* continue, why may we not be of one heart and of one mind? or why should this disagreement break the bonds of good brotherhood?" (Irenicum, Sect. 6.)

The same practical concession was made by the Rev. Bishop Davenant, another of the delegates to the Synod of Dort, from the Church of England. After his return from that Synod, and after his advancement to the bishopric of Salisbury, he published a work in which he urged, with much earnestness and force, a fraternal union among all the Reformed Churches;—a plan which involved an explicit acknowledgment that the Reformed Churches, most of which were Presbyterian, were true Churches of Christ, and which, indeed, contained in its very title a declaration that these churches "did not differ from the Church of England in any fundamental article of Christian faith." The title of the work is as follows: "*Ad Fraternam Communionem inter Evangelicas Ecclesias restaurandam Adhortatio; in eo fundata, quod non dissentiant in ullo fundamentali Catholicæ fidei articulo.*" (*Cantab.* 1640.)

But to return to the Synod of Dort. It was opened on the 13th of November, 1618. John Bogerman, one of the deputies from Friesland, was chosen moderator, or president; and Jacobus Rolandus, one of the ministers of Amsterdam, and Herman Faukelius, minister of Middleburg, his assessors, or assistants. The two secretaries were Sebastian Dammannus, minister of Zutphen, and Festus Hommius, minister of Leyden.

Each of the members of the Synod, before proceeding to business, took the following solemn oath, or engagement: "I promise before God, in whom I believe, and whom I worship, as being present in this place, and as being the Searcher of all hearts, that during the course of the proceedings of this Synod, which will examine and decide, not only the five points, and all the differences resulting from them, but also any other doctrine, I will use no human writing, but only the word of God, which is an infallible rule of faith. And during all these discussions, I will only aim at the glory of God, the peace of the church, and especially the preservation of the purity of doctrine. So help me, my Saviour, Jesus Christ! I beseech him to assist me by his Holy Spirit!"

It was some time before the delegates of the Remonstrants, or Arminian party, made their appearance. At the twenty-second session of the Synod, Episcopius, and his twelve colleagues, who had been summoned for this purpose, presented themselves to make their explanation and defence. In undertaking this task, they manifested the same disposition to delay, to elude inquiry, and to throw obstacles in the way of every plan of proceeding that was proposed. Episcopius was their chief speaker; and with great art and address did he manage their cause. He insisted on being permitted to begin with a refutation of the Calvinistic doctrines, especially that of reprobation, hoping that, by placing his objections to this doctrine in front of all the rest, he might excite such prejudice against the other articles of the system, as to secure the popular voice in his favour. The Synod, however, very properly, reminded him that they had not convened for the purpose of trying the Confession of Faith of the Belgic Churches, which had been long established and well known; but that, as the Remonstrants were accused of departing from the Reformed faith, they were bound *first to justify themselves*, by giving Scriptural proof in support of their opinions.

To this plan of procedure they would by no means submit. It disconcerted their whole scheme; but the Synod firmly refused to adopt any other plan. This refusal, of course, shut the Remonstrants out from taking any part in the deliberations of the body. Day after day they were reasoned with, and urged to submit to a course of proceeding ecclesiastically regular, and adapted to their situation, but without success. They were, therefore, compelled to withdraw. Upon their departure, the Synod proceeded without them.

The language of the President (Bogerman) in dismissing the Remonstrants was rough, and adapted to give pain. He pointedly charged them with fraudulent proceedings, with disingenuous acts, with falsehood, &c. For this language, however, he alone was responsible. It had not been dictated or authorized by the Synod. And a number of the members, we are assured, heard it with regret, and expressed their disapprobation of it. (Hales's Works, vol. iii. p. 123) And yet, while this language was severe, and for an ecclesiastical assembly unseemly, was it not substantially according to truth?

The Synod does not appear to have accomplished its work by referring different portions of it to different committees; but the plan adopted was to request the divines from each country represented in the Synod to consult together, and bring in their separate opinions or judgments in regard to the main points in controversy. So that the sentence, or opinion of the Dutch divines, of the English divines, of the Genevese divines, &c. &c., were separately obtained, and distinctly recorded in the proceedings of the Synod. This method of conducting the business was probably less favourable to dispassionate and perfectly calm proceedings than if committees had matured in private every part of the work.

The Synod examined the Arminian tenets, condemned them as unscriptural, pestilential errors, and pronounced those who held and published them to be enemies of the faith of the Belgic churches, and corrupters of the true religion. They also deposed the Arminian ministers, excluded them and their followers from the communion of the church, suppressed their religious assemblies, and by the aid of the civil government, which confirmed all their acts, sent a number of the clergy of that party, and of those who adhered to them, into banishment. From a large part of their disabilities, however, the Remonstrants, after the lapse of a few years, were relieved.

It is probable that all impartial persons, who make up an opinion with that light, and those habits of thinking with regard to religious liberty which we now possess, will judge that some of these proceedings were by far too harsh and violent. To suppress the religious assemblies of the Remonstrants, by secular authority, and to banish their leaders from their country, were measures which we cannot, at this day, contemplate but with deep regret, as inconsistent with those rights of conscience which we must regard as indefeasible. But when we consider that those rights were really understood by no branch of the

Christian Church at that day; when we recollect that in the Church of England, during the reign of the same James I., who sent representatives to this Synod, more than twenty persons were put to death for their religion, at least two of whom were burnt alive, viz.: Bartholomew Legate, at Smithfield, by the direct influence of Dr. King, Bishop of London, and Edward Wightman, at Litchfield, by the equally direct influence of Bishop Neill, of Litchfield and Coventry; and that many hundreds were banished their country;—and when we recollect that even the pious Puritans, who migrated from their own country to America, that they might enjoy religious liberty, persecuted, in their turn, even unto death for the sake of religion; and especially when we remember the disingenuous, provoking, unworthy course by which the Remonstrants had divided and agitated the Belgic Churches for a number of years, and also the highly unbecoming language which they employed even before the Synod;* when all these things are considered, it is presumed no impartial man will wonder, though he may weep, at some of the proceedings of that far-famed and venerable Synod. After all, however, there can be no doubt that a large part of the violence popularly ascribed to that Synod existed only in the imaginations, the complaints, and the books of the Remonstrants, who were not, of course, impartial judges. The learning, piety, and venerable character of the great and good men who composed it, ought to be considered as an ample guaranty of the decorum of their proceedings. But, more than

* See Hales's Letters from the Synod of Dort, Vol. III. pp. 69, 80, 101, &c.

this, if the Synod had not been entirely decent in its mode of conducting business, can we imagine that Bishop Hall, one of the English delegates, a man remarkable for the piety, benevolence, and amiableness of his character, would have said, "There was no place upon earth which he regarded as so like heaven as the Synod of Dort, or in which he should be more glad to remain?" Surely the testimony of such a man is more worthy of confidence than the statements of men who were smarting under the discipline of the Synod.

I have said that the Synod condemned the Remonstrants. In this they were unanimous. The Canons of the Synod, which contain their decisions with regard to the five Arminian articles, and which are presented in this volume, were adopted without a dissenting voice. We are not, however, to suppose from this fact, that all the members of the Synod were entirely of one mind in regard to all the points embraced in those articles. This was by no means the case. There was much warm discussion during the transactions of the Synod. Some members of the body, such as Gomarus, and others, were advocates of the most high-toned supralapsarian Calvinism; while another portion of the members were not disposed to go further than the sublapsarian hypothesis; and though all agreed in condemning the Remonstrants, yet a very small number of the delegates appear to have occupied ground not very different from that which we commonly call Baxterian. The Canons, however, were such as they could all unite in. The praise which Dr. Scott bestows on the Formulary of Faith drawn up by the Synod, as a wise, moderate, well digested, and well expressed exhibition of theological principles, is well merited. It is worthy of high commendation. It must be confessed, indeed, that, as a monument of ecclesiastical wisdom, taste, sound learning, judgment, and singular comprehensiveness, the results of the Westminster Assembly, a few years afterwards, not a little exceed those of Dort; but the latter stand next in order, on the scale of Synodical labours. Among all the uninspired theological compositions of the seventeenth century, many of the best judges are of the opinion that the "Confession of Faith" and "Catechisms" framed by the Westminster Assembly hold the very highest place. The writer of this page is free to confess that he has never seen any human document of that age, or indeed of any other, public or private, which in his estimation is quite equal to them for the purpose which they were destined to answer.

The Synod of Dort continued to sit from the 13th of November, A. D. 1618, to the 29th of May, 1619. It held, in all, one hundred and eighty sittings; and was conducted entirely at the expense of the States General.

Dr. Mosheim speaks with more than his usual candour when he treats of the heat and violence which broke out, on various occasions, in Holland, in the course of the Arminian controversy; and especially of the political animosity which unfortunately became intimately connected with that theological and ecclesiastical dispute, and which led to the beheading of Oldenbarneveldt, and to the banishment of Grotius, Hoogerbeets, and others. The truth is, in a number of cases the political aspect of the subject became the prominent one. The consequence was, that many men became implicated in it who laid no claim to piety; hence the frequency with which the affair had the appearance of a contest among politicians rather than Christians. Still it is believed that even these secular struggles have been magnified for the sake of blackening the anti-Arminian body, who happened to be connected with the strongest political party.

In the Church of Holland, the majority against the Remonstrants, and in favour of orthodoxy, was very large. Judging from the number of ministers reckoned in the established church, and among the Remonstrants, the latter did not constitute more than a thirtieth part of the population. And the proportion remains pretty much the same still: for although since that time the number is greatly increased among the ministers of the Dutch churches, of those who embrace Pelagian and Semi-Pelagian sentiments, yet many who agree with the Remonstrants in doctrinal opinions, and even some who go much farther in heresy than they, do not take their name, or unite with their societies, as the Remonstrants labour under civil disabilities, which multitudes who substantially agree with them in sentiment do not choose to incur by openly joining their ranks.

After the death of the Prince of Orange, A. D. 1625, the Remonstrants began to be treated more mildly. The ministers were recalled from their banishment, and restored to their functions and churches; and from that period to the present have been tolerated in the United Provinces, and more lately, since the change of government, in the kingdom of Holland. Indeed, it is melancholy to say, that for a number of years past, in the kingdom of Holland, Pelagian and Unitarian sentiments have obtained such currency in the church of that country, that the only difficulty has been for the friends of truth to obtain permission to preach, unobstructed, the pure Gospel.

Although the many and great evils which always result from the civil establishment of religion, may not have been so strongly exemplified in the Church of Holland, as in some other countries, yet through the whole of the controversy now in question, as well as on various occasions since, we have seen that this unhallowed connection, however coveted by worldly minded ecclesiastics, in all cases stands in the way of the simple and pure dispensation of the Gospel, and never fails to be a curse rather than a blessing. And this, we may confidently say, has been substantially the judgment of the best men in all ages in which any just sentiments on this subject have prevailed or been cherished at all. Mr. Gibbon, if I mistake not, has somewhere observed, with a sarcastic sneer, that he is sorry to say, that the earliest and most zealous advocates of religious liberty have ever been *laymen*, and not ministers of religion. However well-informed that learned infidel may have been on other subjects, he is here under a mistake, which, however, may be easily accounted for. The character of his mind, and the habits of his life, led him to a much more intimate acquaintance with the writings of laymen and worldly-minded ecclesiastics, than with the works of evangelical and orthodox ministers. No wonder, then, that he was ignorant of some testimony on this subject, which, had he been acquainted with it, would have led to a different judgment. When the Priscillianists, in the fourth century, were persecuted and delivered over to the secular arm to be punished with death, who lamented and opposed the cruel oppression which they endured? Martin, Bishop of Tours, an eminently pious man, with a number of others of like spirit, mourned over the treatment which they received, remonstrated against it, and pronounced it a *novum et inauditum nefas.* And in regard to the writers on the subject of religious liberty in the seventeenth century, to whom there was probably a special reference in the remark which it now combatted, the simplest statement of facts will show that the earliest and most thorough-going advocates of religious liberty, at that period, were all ecclesiastical men; and all of that class with which Mr. Gibbon would be neither likely nor disposed to have much acquaintance.

In 1614, the Rev. Leonard Busher, a zealous Brownist, or ultra Independent minister, presented to king James I. and his parliament, "Religious Peace, or a Plea for Liberty of Conscience." The leading object of this treatise is to show, that the true way to make a nation happy is, "to give liberty to all to serve God according as they are persuaded is most agreeable to his word; to speak, write, print, peaceably and without molestation in behalf of their several tenets and ways of worship." In a few years afterwards, the Rev. John Robinson, a divine of the Church of England, who had been bred at the University of Cambridge, and fled from persecution in his native country to Holland, where he cast in his lot with the Independents, published two works, one entitled "A Justification of Separation from the Church of England;" and another in explanation and defence of the first, entitled "A Just and Necessarie Apologie," &c. In these works he contended with no small force, both of learning and argument, that Christ's kingdom is not of this world; —that it is entirely spiritual, and he its spiritual King; and that civil magistrates have no right to interfere, in any wise, or in any case, with liberty of conscience. In

1644, the celebrated Roger Williams, a native of England, a graduate of the University of Oxford, who had received orders in the Established Church of England, who came to New England in 1630, and there cast in his lot with the Independents, and ultimately becoming a Baptist, withdrew from Massachusetts to Rhode Island, where he became the pastor of the first Baptist church in the American Colonies, and established a separate government, published a work under the following title—"The Bloody Tenet of Persecution for the cause of Conscience," in which he plead for liberty of conscience on the broadest and most liberal principles. In short, he carried the doctrine to the utmost length, and maintained that the civil magistrate has no right to enforce any of the precepts contained in the first table of the Decalogue. And, what is still more to the honour of Roger Williams, as he was, in a sort, the civil ruler, as well as the spiritual guide, of the colony of Rhode Island, it deserves to be recorded that he was the first Governor who ever practically acknowledged that complete liberty of conscience was the birthright of man, and who really and consistently yielded it to those who widely differed from him, when he had the full power to withhold it.

In 1649, the Rev. Dr. John Owen, educated in the University of Oxford, and afterwards Vice-Chancellor of that University, universally known to have been an eminent Independent minister, and one of the greatest theologians of his age, published a work on "Toleration," which does honour to his memory, and deserves to be ranked among the best publications on that subject. He does not, indeed, in his theory, go quite so far as Roger Williams; yet he explicitly states, and by a variety of arguments maintains, that "the civil magistrate has no right to meddle with the religion of any person whose conduct is not injurious to society, and destructive of its peace and order." And it ought to be stated, to the honour of this great and good man, that he acted on the principles which he had avowed, when his own party was triumphant, and he had it in his power to oppress. It is also further worthy of notice, that, some years after the publication of this work, when the Puritans in New England were, most inconsistently, persecuting the Baptists and Quakers, Dr. Owen, at the head of a body of Nonconformist ministers in London, sent an address to them, remonstrating against their conduct, and entreating them to cease from their persecuting measures, which, accordingly, they soon did. The language of this address is striking and to the point. Among other things it is said—"We make it our hearty request, that you will trust God with his truth and ways, so far as to suspend all rigorous proceedings in corporeal restraints or punishments on persons that dissent from you, and practise the principles of their dissent, without danger or disturbance to the civil peace."

Perhaps the learned reader will be apt to ask why the name of Bishop Jeremy Taylor has not a place assigned in this list of advocates for religious liberty. The reason for not giving him a conspicuous place in this honoured catalogue, will appear from the following statement. In the year 1647, that great and eloquent man, who has been strongly styled "the Shakspeare of the English pulpit," published his "Liberty of Prophesying," in which a great deal of important truth on this subject is communicated, with a power for which the author was distinguished in all his works. The writer, however, argues chiefly from considerations which do not hold a legitimate, and certainly not a primary place among the controlling arguments on this subject. For example, he reasons in favour of religious liberty, from the difficulty of expounding the Scriptures so as to arrive at any certain conclusion on some points; from the incompetency of Popes, Councils, or the church at large, to determine articles of faith; from the innocence of error, where there is real piety; and from the antiquity and plausibility of various sentiments and practices generally held to be erroneous. It is more on such grounds as these that he rests his defence of toleration, than on the inherent and essential rights of men, and the authority of the word of God. Such an advocate can scarcely be recognized as pleading for the same principles with Williams, Owen, and his other clerical contemporaries in the same nominal field.

But there is another, and still more serious objection to our assigning to Jeremy Taylor an honourable place in the list of early and able advocates of religious liberty. When he wrote his work on the "Liberty of Prophesying," he and his church were under the frown of government. He was, in fact, pleading for toleration for himself and for Episcopacy. When Charles II. was restored to the throne; when Taylor came forth from retirement and oppression; and when he was raised to the Episcopate, he consented to become a member of the privy council of that faithless and profligate monarch, from which so many persecuting edicts against the non-conformists issued, to the disgrace of their authors. And even if it be doubted whether he ever took any active part in the persecuting edicts of that monarch, as a member of his council, yet it is notorious and unquestionable, that in his diocese in Ireland, he was chargeable with much and severe persecution. If he ever entertained correct sentiments in respect to the rights of conscience, he forgot or disregarded them all when he rose to power, and was enabled to persecute. (See Orme's Life of Owen, p. 101; and the History of the Presbyterian Church in Ireland, by James Seaton Reid, D. D. M. R. S. A. p. 344, &c.)

While justice is done to the ministers of the gospel above mentioned, I have no desire to derogate, in the least degree, from the credit due to Milton* and Locke,† of the same century, whom it is the fashion to eulogize as the great pioneers in pleading for religious liberty. There is no doubt that both these illustrious laymen wrote nobly in defence of the cause in question; and that both ought to be held in grateful remembrance for their noble services; yet it is surely wrong to ascribe to them, meritorious as they were, all the credit of originating a doctrine which had been held, and publicly defended many years, before either of them had published or written a line on the subject.

The National Synod of Holland has never met since the adjournment of the Synod of Dort, in 1619. By the fiftieth article of the Rules of Government which that Synod adopted, it was prescribed that a general Synod should meet every three years, but not without the approbation of the civil government. This article, however, has never been carried into effect, either because the

* Milton's work, entitled "A Treatise of Civil Power in Ecclesiastical Causes," was published in 1659.

† Locke's first Letter on Toleration was published, in Holland, in the Latin language, in 1689.

magistrates have withheld their consent, or because the Church has never asked the necessary permission. The original manuscript of the "Acts of the Synod of Dort," having been put into the possession of the States General, they, in the year 1625, resolved that that manuscript should, *every three years*, be inspected by delegates from their own body, and deputies from the provincial Synods jointly. Accordingly, this ceremony, we are told, is gone through, with a punctilious formality, in the month of May of every third year. Twenty-two deputies from the Synods repair to the Hague, where they are joined by two delegates of the secular government. This joint body then proceeds to the public chamber in which the chest containing the Acts of the Synod is deposited. This chest is opened with eight several keys. The Acts, which are neatly bound up in seventeen volumes, are formally taken out and shown, first to the governmental delegates, and then to the clerical members of the body. This ceremony is preceded and followed with prayer, after which the members of the inspecting committee dine together, and thus terminates their triennial task.

The venerable Dr. Scott was prompted, he tells us, to undertake the translation of the official history and cannons of the Synod of Dort, by the persuasion that they had been greatly misapprehended by the religious public, in which he had himself, for many years, largely participated. The truth is, the misrepresentations of the proceedings of that Synod by Peter Heylin, and Daniel Tilenus, are so gross and shameful, that it is difficult adequately to animadvert upon them in strictly temperate language. As to Peter Heylin, he hardly knew how to speak the truth when Calvinism or Presbyterianism was in question. And, with respect to Daniel Tilenus, who was a theological Professor in the Presbyterian seminary at Sedan, in France, and had been once a Calvinist, but afterwards joined the Arminian ranks, his prejudices against his old opinions became, after his apostacy, so perfectly bitter and blinding, that he seemed incapable of representing them otherwise than under the most revolting caricature. No wonder that those who believed these men, regarded the Acts of the Synod with abhorrence. Dr. Scott, as the reader will perceive, declares himself satisfied, that the proceedings of the Synod had been greatly and criminally slandered; that their canons were among the most Scriptural and excellent formularies he had ever seen; and that he thought it incumbent on him to do all in his power to remove the veil from the false statements concerning them, which had been so confidently made, and to the circulation of which he had himself, in some degree, unintentionally contributed.

This translation was among the last works, if not the very last, which Dr. Scott gave to the public. It was published only a few months prior to his decease, and was prepared by him under an immediate impression of that solemn account which he was so nearly approaching, and of the duty which he owed to the public in behalf of a greatly injured body.

The following remarks of Mons. Bayle, in his Biographical Dictionary, under the article Arminius, are so apposite and pointed as to form a very appropriate extract for this Introductory Essay. Bayle himself was, probably, neither a Calvinist nor an Arminian, but a cool, insidious sceptic. His judgment, therefore, on this controversy, may be considered as the decision of a shrewd, and, as to this point, an impartial mind, on a matter concerning which he had no point to gain, or party to serve.

"It were to be wished that he (Arminius) had made a better use of his knowledge. I mean, that he had governed himself by St. Paul's rule. This great apostle, immediately inspired by God, and directed by the Holy Ghost in all his writings, raised to himself the objection which the light of nature forms against the doctrine of absolute predestination. He apprehended the whole force of the objection, and he proposes it without weakening it in the least degree. *God hath mercy on whom he will have mercy, and whom he will he hardeneth.* Rom. ix. 18. This is Paul's doctrine, and the difficulty which he starts upon it is this—*Thou wilt say then unto me, Why doth he yet find fault, for who hath resisted his will?* This objection cannot be pushed further; twenty pages, by the most subtile Molinist, could add nothing to it. What more could they infer than that, upon Calvin's hypothesis, God wills men to commit sin? Now this is what St. Paul knew might be objected against him; but what does he reply? Does he seek for distinctions and qualifications? Does he deny the fact? Does he grant it in part only? Does he enter into particulars? Does he remove any ambiguity in the words? Nothing of all this. He only alleges the sovereign power of God, and the supreme right which the Creator has to dispose of his creatures as it seems good to him. *Nay, but O man, who art thou that repliest against God!* He acknowledges an incomprehensibility in the thing which ought to put a stop to all disputes, and to impose a profound silence on our reason. He cries out, *O the depth of the riches, both of the wisdom and knowledge of God!*

How unsearchable are his judgments, and his ways are past finding out. All Christians ought to find here a definite sentence, a judgment final, and without appeal in the dispute about grace. Or rather, they should learn from this conduct of St. Paul, never to dispute about predestination, and immediately to oppose this bar against all the subtleties of human wit, whether they arise of themselves, in meditating on this great subject, or whether others suggest them. The best and the shortest way is, early to oppose this strong bank against the inundations of reasoning, and to consider this definitive sentence of St. Paul as a rock immovable in the midst of the waves, against which the proudest billows may beat in vain. They may foam and dash, but are only broken against them. All arrows darted against this shield, will have the same fate as that of Priam."

Further on the same writer says:—"To a system full of great difficulties, Arminius has substituted another system, which, to speak truly, involves no less difficulties than the former. One may say of his doctrine what I have observed of the innovations of Saumur. It is better connected and less forced than the opinions of Mr. Amyraut; but, after all, it is but a palliative remedy, for the Arminians have scarcely been able to answer some objections which, as they pretend, cannot be refuted upon Calvin's system. Besides, they find themselves exposed to other difficulties which they cannot get over but by an ingenuous confession of the weakness of human reason, and the consideration of the incomprehensible infinity of God. And was it worth while to contradict Calvin for this? Why was Arminius so very difficult at first, when at last he was obliged to fly to this asylum?

Why did he not begin here, since here he must come, sooner or later? He is mistaken who imagines that, after entering the lists with a great disputant, he shall be allowed to triumph only for some small advantage which he had over him at first. An athlete, who throws out his antagonist in the middle of the race, but has not the advantage of him at the end, is not entitled to the palm. It is the same in controversy. It is not sufficient to parry the first thrusts. Every reply and rejoinder must be satisfied, and every doubt perfectly cleared up. Now this is what neither the hypothesis of Arminius, nor that of the Molinists, nor that of the Socinians, is able to do. The system of the Arminians is only calculated to give some few advantages in those preludes to war, in which the forlorn hope is sent out to skirmish. But when it comes to a general and decisive battle, this detachment must retire, as well as the rest, behind the intrenchments of incomprehensible mystery."

Perhaps it may be said, that no theological system was ever more grossly misrepresented, or more foully or unjustly vilified, than that which is commonly called Calvinism, but which has been drawn from the word of God, and preached by some of the best men that ever lived, many hundreds of years before Calvin was born. The truth is, it would be difficult to name a writer or speaker who has distinguished himself by opposing this system, who has fairly represented it, or who really appeared to understand it. They are for ever fighting against an imaginary monster of their own creation. They picture to themselves the consequences which they suppose unavoidably flow from the real principles of Calvinists, and then, most unjustly, represent these consequences as a part of the system itself, as held by its advocates. Whether this arises from the want of knowledge, or the want of candour, is not for me to decide; but the effect is the same, and the conduct worthy of severe censure. How many an eloquent page of anti-Calvinistic declamation would be instantly seen by every reader to be either calumny or nonsense, if it had been preceded by an honest statement of what the system, as held by Calvinists, really is.

The enemies of the system allege, that it represents God as really the author of sin, and man as laid under a physical necessity of sinning, and then as damned for it, do what he can. They insist that our doctrine of *depravity*, and the mode of inheriting it, if true, destroys moral agency, reduces men to the condition of mere machines, and, of course, makes all punishment of sin unjust and absurd. In short, they contend that the views which we give of the plan of salvation, makes a system of heathenish fate, or of refined Antinomianism, equally destructive of holiness and of comfort; and that, under the guise of free grace, we build up a fabric of favouritism on the one hand, and of fixed necessity on the other; at once making God a partial being and a tyrant, and man a mere passive subject of his arbitrary will. But is it true that Calvinists embrace any such system as this? Nothing can be further from the truth. It is a shameful misrepresentation, which has no correspondence with any thing but the caricatures of prejudice and bigotry. Calvinists abhor such sentiments just as much as their uncandid accusers do. Many wise and excellent men have been of the opinion that Arminian principles, when traced out to their natural and unavoidable consequences, lead to an invasion of the essential attributes of God, and, of course, to blank and cheerless atheism. Yet, in making a statement of the Arminian system, as actually held by its advocates, what candid man would allow himself to introduce into the delineation any thing different from or beyond the actual admissions of those advocates? The system itself is one thing; the consequences which may be drawn from it, another.

It is not pretended that the Calvinistic system is free from all difficulties. When finite creatures are called to scan either the works or the revealed will of an Infinite Being, they must be truly demented if they expect to find nothing which is incomprehensible. Accordingly, when we undertake to solve some of the difficulties which the Calvinistic system presents, it cannot be denied that "such knowledge is too wonderful for us; it is high, we cannot attain unto it." How to reconcile what the Scriptures plainly reveal, on the hand, concerning the entire dependence of man; and, on the other, concerning his activity and responsibility; how to explain the perfect foreknowledge and predestination of God, in consistency with the perfect freedom and moral agency of his intelligent creatures, is a problem which no thinking man expects fully to solve. But the question is, Are there fewer difficulties attending any other system? Especially are there fewer difficulties attending the Arminian or Pelagian system, one or the other of which is usually the resort of those who reject Calvinism? There are not; nay, instead of being less, they are greater—far greater both in number and magnitude. For example, it is easy, and, in the estimation of the superficial and unreflecting, it appears conclusive, to object, that Calvinism has a tendency to cut the nerves of all spiritual exertion; that if we are elected, we shall be saved, do what we will; and if not elected, we shall be lost, do what we can. But is it not perfectly evident that the objection here lies with quite as much force against the Arminian or Pelagian hypothesis? Arminians and Pelagians both grant that all men will not actually be saved; that the salvation or perdition of each individual is distinctly foreknown by God; and that the event will certainly happen as he foresees that it will. May not a caviller, then, say, with quite as much appearance of justice in this case as in the other, "The result, as to my salvation, though unknown to me, is known to God, and certain. If I am to be saved, no anxiety about it is necessary; and if I am to perish, all anxiety about it would be useless." But would an Arminian consider such an objection as valid against his creed? Probably not. Yet it is certainly just as valid against his creed as against ours. The truth is, the Arminian, by resorting to his scheme, does not really get rid of one particle of the difficulty which he alleges against the Calvinistic system: he only places it one step further back, but must meet it in its full strength after all. Until we can bring ourselves to swallow the monstrous absurdity, that what is to be, will not be; that what God foresees as certain, may never happen, the cavil, such as it is, remains unanswered. If there be a God who is endowed with perfect foreknowledge, and who is, and always has been, acting upon a plan, of which he knows the end from the beginning—and there is such a Being, or there is no God;—then all the difficulty which lies against the doctrine of sovereign, unconditional predetermination, lies equally, and in all its unmitigated force, against the doctrine of foreknowledge and certain futurition, in any form that can be imagined; and all the shocking consequences with which they charge Calvinism, are quite as legitimately chargeable against any and every scheme, short of atheism, which may be embraced to get rid of them.

No other proof of this is needed than the subterfuges to which Arminians and Pelagians have resorted in order to obviate the objections which they have felt pressing on their respective schemes. Some have denied the possibility of God's foreknowing future contingencies; alleging that such foreknowledge cannot be conceived or admitted, more than the power of doing impossibilities, or doing what involves a contradiction. Others have denied the plenary foreknowledge of God altogether; alleging that there are many things which he does not choose to know;—the latter making the divine ignorance of many future things voluntary, while the former consider it as necessary. A third class, to get rid of the same difficulties, take refuge in the principle that the Most High is deficient in power as well as in knowledge; that his plan—so far as he has any—is continually thwarted and opposed beyond his power of control; that he would be glad to have less natural and moral evil in his kingdom than exists; would be glad to have many more saved than will be saved; but is not able to fulfil his wishes, and is constantly restrained and defeated by his own creatures!

Do not these boasted refuges from Calvinism shock every mind not thoroughly hardened and profane? Do not the allegations that God is not omnipotent; that he is not omniscient; that he is not acting upon an eternal and settled plan; that his purposes, instead of being eternal, are all formed in time; and instead of being immutable, are all liable to be altered every day, and are, in fact, altered by the changing will of his creatures; that there is no certainty of his predictions and promises ever being fulfilled, because he can neither foresee nor control future contingencies; that it is his express design to save all men alike, while yet it is certain that all will not be saved; that he purposes as much, and does as much for those who perish, as for those who are saved; but is, after all, baffled and disappointed in his hopes concerning them; that he is certain of nothing, because he has determined on nothing positively, and if he had is not able to do all his pleasure—do not such allegations fill every thinking mind with horror? Are they not equally contrary to Scripture, to reason, and to all the hopes and consolations of the pious? Would not such a God, with reverence be it spoken, be the most unhappy being in the universe? True, indeed, Arminians do not recognize these horrid consequences, and therefore cannot be charged with holding them; but they are not, on this account, the less inevitable, or the less awful.

But though that system of grace, usually denominated Calvinism, is now in such bad odour with multitudes in the Church of England, and with many connected with her ecclesiastical daughter in this country—it was not always so. When the Synod of Dort convened, the same theological system which that celebrated Synod sustained, was the reigning creed in the Church of England, and had been so, beyond all question, for more than half a century. This has, indeed, been denied; but it would be just as reasonable to deny that such men as Cranmer, and Whitgift, and Hooker, and Hall, and Usher, ever occupied stations in the established Church of that land. Testimony to establish the position which has been assumed, which prejudice itself cannot refute, crowds upon us, and offers itself on every side.

The testimony of Peter Heylin, a bitter enemy to Calvinism, is clear and decisive. "It cannot be denied," says he, "but that, by the error of these times, the reputation which Calvin had attained to in both Universities, and the extreme diligence of his followers, there was a general tendency unto his opinions; his book of Institutes being, for the most part, the foundation on which the young divines of those days did build their studies." Again he declares—"Of any men who publicly opposed the Calvinian tenets in the University of Oxford, till after the beginning of king James's reign, I must confess that I have hitherto found no good assurance." He speaks of two divines of inferior note, who secretly propagated Arminian principles; and compares them to the prophet Elijah, who considered himself as left alone to oppose a whole world of idolaters. Further: in the reign of Charles I., more than sixty years after the final settling of the thirty-nine Articles, when a suppression of the Calvinistic doctrines was contemplated by Archbishop Laud, Heylin acknowledges that such was the general attachment of the bishops and clergy to these doctrines, that the Arminian party did not dare to "venture the determining of these points to a Convocation."* And he again explicitly informs us, that, from the re-settling of the Church under Queen Elizabeth, to the period already mentioned, "the maintainers of the anti-Calvinian doc-

* See Heylin's Quinq. Hist. Work, p. 626, &c. See also his Life of Laud, p. 147.

trines were few in number, and made but a very thin appearance."

The famous Lambeth Articles, drawn up in 1595, during the reign of Queen Elizabeth, are acknowledged by all who ever read them, to be among the most strongly marked Calvinistical compositions that ever were penned. They were drawn up by Archbishop Whitgift, then at the head of the English Established Church, and one of its most conspicuous divines and fathers. The archbishop was assisted in this service by the bishops of London and Bangor, and by some others. After receiving the public approbation of these dignitaries, the Articles were sent to the Archbishop of York, and the Bishop of Rochester, who also subscribed them. Thus ratified, Archbishop Whitgift sent them to the University of Cambridge, with a letter, in which he declared—"That these Articles were not to be considered as laws and decrees, but as propositions which he and his brethren were persuaded were true, and corresponding with the doctrine professed in the Church of England, and established by the laws of the land." Nor is this all: it having been suggested by some, that the Archbishop agreed to these Articles rather for the sake of peace, than because he believed them, Strype, his Episcopal biographer, repels the charge with indignation, declaring that such an insinuation is as false as it is mean and disparaging to the primate.*

Not long after the delegates to the Synod of Dort, from the Church of England, returned home, they were attacked by certain writers, who reproached them for having signed the Articles of the Synod, and charged them with having, by that act, given countenance to error, and also with having departed from the Articles of their own

* Strype's Life of Whitgift, pp. 461—463.

Church. Against this attack they thought proper to defend themselves, by what they called a joint attestation, which contains the following passage: "Whatsoever there was assented unto, and subscribed by us, concerning the five Articles, either in the joint Synodical judgment, or in our particular collegiate suffrage, is not only warrantable by the holy Scriptures, but also conformable to the received doctrine of our said venerable mother, which we are ready to maintain and justify against all gainsayers."

Again, Bishop Hall, before mentioned as one of the delegates, in a work of his own, addressed to some who had charged him, and some other bishops of his day, with entertaining Arminian sentiments as to the doctrine of election, thus indignantly replies to the charge: "You add, 'election upon faith foreseen.' What! nothing but gross untruths? Is this the doctrine of the bishops of England? Have they not strongly confuted it, in Papists and Arminians? Have they not cried it down to the lowest pit of hell?" *

The same pious prelate himself tells us, that after his return from the Synod of Dort, where he had been, as we have seen, an advocate of Calvinistic doctrine, and a warm and open opponent of Arminianism, he was distressed to find that heresy gaining ground in England. "Not many years," says he, "after settling at home, it grieved my soul to see our own church begin to sicken of the same disease, which we had endeavoured to cure in our neighbours."†

---

* Defence of the Humble Remonstrance. Works, vol. iii. p. 246.

† Some Specialties of the Life of Joseph Hall, Bishop of Norwich, written by himself, prefixed to the third volume of his works.

That the thirty-nine Articles of the Church of England are Calvinistic, has been so often asserted and demonstrated, that a new attempt to establish the fact is certainly unnecessary. The seventeenth Article in particular, bears ample testimony to this fact. I am aware, indeed, that it has been alleged, that the qualifying clause toward the end of the Article, shows that the framers of it meant to reject Calvinism. Now it so happens that the very qualifying clause in question, is nearly copied from Calvin's Institutes, and the latter part of that clause is a literal translation of that Reformer's caution against the abuse of this doctrine. For evidence of the former, see his Institutes III. 21, 4, 5, compared with the Article, where every idea contained in that part of the Article will be found recited. For proof of the latter, read the following: "*Proinde, in rebus agendis, ea est nobis perspicienda Dei voluntas quam verbo suo declarat.*" Instit. I. 17, 5. "Furthermore, in our doings, that will of God is to be followed, which we have expressly declared to us in the word of God." Art. 17th.*

A correspondent of the Christian Observer, a clergyman of the Established Church of England, in speaking of the disposition of many in his own church, to vilify the name and opinions of Calvin, makes the following remarks:

"Few names stand higher, or in more deserved preeminence, among the wise and pious members of the English Church, than that of Bishop Andrews. His testimony to the memory of Calvin is, that he was 'an

* For this reference, to show that the 17th Article is not to be interpreted as opposed to Calvinism, see Christian Observer, of London, vol. iii. p. 438.

illustrious person, and never to be mentioned without a preface of the highest honour.' Whoever examines into the sermons, writings, &c., of our divines in the reign of Elizabeth, and James I., will continually meet with epithets of honour with which his name is mentioned; the learned, the wise, the judicious, the pious Calvin, are expressions everywhere to be found in the remains of those times. It is well known that his Institutes were read and studied in the universities, by every student in divinity; nay, that, by a convocation held at Oxford, that book was recommended to the general study of the nation. So far were the Church of England, and her chief divines, from countenancing that unbecoming and absurd treatment with which the name of this eminent Protestant is now so frequently dishonoured, that it would be no difficult matter to prove, that there is not, perhaps, a parallel instance upon record, of any single individual being equally, and so unequivocally venerated, for the union of wisdom and piety, both in England and by a large body of the foreign churches, as John Calvin. Nothing but ignorance of the ecclesiastical records of those times, or resolute prejudice, could cast a cloak of concealment over this fact. It has been evidenced by the combined testimony both of enemies and friends to his system of doctrines."*

PRINCETON, May, 1841.

---

* Christian Observer, vol. ii. p. 143.

PREFACE.

THE manner in which the author was brought to the determination of adding the present work to all his former publications, will appear more fully in the introduction to the articles of the Synod of Dordrecht, or Dort. In general, he had erroneously adopted, and aided in circulating, a gross misrepresentation of the Synod and its decisions, in his "Remarks on the Refutation of Calvinism;" and having discovered his mistake previously to the publication of a second edition of that work, he was induced to do what he could to counteract that misrepresentation, and to vindicate the Synod from the atrocious calumnies, with which it has been wilfully or inadvertently traduced. But other motives concurred in disposing him to give his attempt its present form and order.

1. A very interesting and important part of ecclesiastical history has been obscured and overwhelmed in unmerited disgrace, by the misrepresentations given of this Synod and its articles, especially in this nation; in which very few, even among studious men, know accurately the circumstances which led to the convening of this Synod, and the real nature and import of its decisions. To excite therefore others, more conversant in these studies, and better qualified for the service, to examine this part of ecclesiastical history, and to do impartial justice to it, is one object which the author has in view.

2. He purposes to prove, that the doctrines commonly

termed Calvinistic, whether they be or be not the doctrines of Scriptural Christianity, may yet be so stated and explained, without any skilful or laboured efforts, as to coincide with the strictest practical views of our holy religion; and so as greatly to encourage and promote genuine holiness, considered in its most expanded nature, and in its effects on all our tempers, affections, words, and actions, in relation to God and to all mankind.

3. In a day when these doctrines are not only proscribed in a most hostile manner on one side, but deplorably misunderstood and perverted by many on the other side, the author desired to add one more testimony against these misapprehensions and perversions, by showing in what a holy, guarded, and reverential manner, the divines of this reprobated Synod stated and explained these doctrines, compared with the superficial, incautious, and often unholy and presumptuous manner of too many in the present day. And if any individual, or a few individuals, should by this publication be induced to employ superior talents and advantages, in counteracting these unscriptural and pernicious statements, his labour will be amply compensated.

4. The author desired to make it manifest, that the deviations from the creeds of the reformed churches, in those points which are more properly called Calvinistic, are seldom for any length of time kept separate from deviations in those doctrines which are more generally allowed to be essential to vital Christianity. It must, indeed, appear from the history with which the work begins, that the progress is easy and almost unavoidable, from the controversial opposition to personal election, to the explaining away of original sin, regeneration by the Holy

Spirit, justification by faith alone, and even of the atonement and Deity of Christ; and that the opponents of the Synod of Dort, and the Remonstrants in general, were far more favourable to Pelagians, nay, to Socinians, than to Calvinists; and were almost universally unsound, in what are commonly called orthodox doctrines, and many of them far from being conscientious in their conduct. Indeed, it will appear undeniable, that the opposition made to them by the Contra-Remonstrants, was much more decidedly on these grounds than because they opposed the doctrine of personal election, and the final perseverance of true believers as connected with it.

5. The author purposed, also, by means of this publication, to leave behind him, in print, his deliberate judgment on several controverted points, which must otherwise have died with him, or have been published separately, for which he had no inclination. But he has here grafted them as notes or remarks on the several parts of this work; and he trusts he has now done with all controversy.

It is doubtless vain to attempt any thing, against many of those opponents who succeed to each other, with sufficient variety, as to the grounds on which they take their stand, and from which they make the assault, but in some respects nearly in the same course of misapprehension, or misrepresentation, as to the real sentiments of those whom they undertake to refute. It suffices to say of them, "Neither can they prove the things of which they accuse us;" and to say to them, "Thou shalt not bear false witness against thy neighbour." But, indeed, Calvinists seem to be no more considered as *neighbours* by many Anti-Calvinists, than the Publicans, Samaritans, and Gentiles, were by the Scribes and Pharisees.

After all that has been published on these subjects, the groundless charges brought by many against the whole body, cannot be considered as excusable misapprehension. They must be either intentional misrepresentation, or the inexcusable presumption of writing on subjects which the writers have never studied, and against persons, and descriptions of persons, of whose tenets, amidst most abundant means of information, they remain wilfully ignorant. A fair and impartial opponent is entitled to respect, but I can only *pity* such controversialists.

THOMAS SCOTT.

ASTON SANFORD, March 15, 1818

THE

PREFACE,

TO THE REFORMED CHURCHES OF CHRIST;

IN WHICH THE RISE AND PROGRESS OF THOSE CONTROVERSIES IN BELGIUM, FOR THE REMOVAL OF WHICH THIS SYNOD WAS ESPECIALLY HELD, ARE BRIEFLY AND FAITHFULLY RELATED.

INTRODUCTION TO THIS PREFACE.

BY THE TRANSLATOR.

In perusing this preface, and the history contained in it, the reader should especially recollect, that it was drawn up and published by the authority and with the sanction of the States General, and the Prince of Orange, as well as by that of the Synod itself; and that, in every part of it, the *acts*, or public records in which the events recorded were registered, are referred to, with the exact dates of each transaction. No history can therefore be attested as authentic, in a more satisfactory and unexceptionable manner; for whatever degree of colouring, prejudices or partiality may be supposed to have given to the narration, it can hardly be conceived, that collective bodies, and individuals filling up such conspicuous and exalted stations, would expressly attest any thing *directly false*; and then appeal to authorities, by which the falsehood of their statement might at any time be detected and exposed. It should also be remembered, that prejudices and partiality would be as likely to colour the account given to the world, and transmitted to posterity by the opposite party; while the very circumstances in which they were placed, would render it impracticable for them to substantiate the authenticity of their narrative in the same manner. Yet, contrary to all rules of a sober and unbiassed judgment, the unauthenticated histories of the Remonstrants* concerning the Synod of Dort, have, almost exclusively, been noticed and credited by posterity, especially in this country, to the neglect of the authentic records.† In giving the translation of this history I would merely say, *Audi alteram partem.* "Do not read the authenticated narration with greater suspicions of unfairness than you do those which are not so fully authenticated. Let not your approbation of what you suppose to have been the doctrine of the Remonstrants, or your aversion to that of the Contra-Remonstrants, bias your mind in this respect, but judge impartially." One of these histories was drawn up by a

---

* So called from a Remonstrance presented by them to the States of Holland and West Friesland, against the doctrines of their opponents, or those of the Federated churches of Belgium.

† Neither Mosheim, nor his translator Maclaine, mentions this history, while they refer to a variety of authorities on both sides of the question, in their narrative of these transactions. So that it is even probable that they had never seen it. Whether the severe measures by which the decisions of this Synod were followed up, and especially the strict prohibition of printing or vending any other account, in Latin, Dutch, or French, in the Federated provinces, during seven years, without a special license for that purpose, did not eventually conduce to this, may be a question. The measure, however, was impolitic, if not unjustifiable.

man (Heylin) who has been fully detected of misrepresenting the very articles of the Synod in the grossest manner, and has thus misled great numbers to mistake entirely the real import and nature of the decision made by it. I appeal to the abbreviation, as it is called, of the Articles of the Synod of Dort, as compared with the real Articles themselves, in another part of this publication. So scandalous a misrepresentation, which has been too implicitly adopted by many others, should render the impartial reader cautious in giving implicit credit to other statements made by the same party, however celebrated the names of some of them may be.

When I first entered on this part of my undertaking, I purposed merely to give a short *abstract* of the history, just enough to render the subsequent part of the work intelligible to the less learned or studious reader; but, whether it were the result of partiality, or of unbiassed judgment, I found myself so deeply interested in the events recorded, (which were almost entirely new to me,) that my reluctance to translating and transcribing the whole was overcome; and (with a few remarks on different parts) I determined to give it entire to the English reader. As far as I am competent to judge it possesses every internal evidence of authenticity and fairness; and of *impartiality*, as far as even pious men, exactly circumstanced as the writers were, in the present imperfect state of human nature, can be expected to be impartial. It is, I think, also drawn up with a degree of calmness and moderation; far different from that fierce and fiery zeal which is generally supposed to belong to all who profess, or are suspected of, what many in a very vague and inappropriate manner call Calvinism. And though according to the *fashion* of those times, epithets are in some instances applied both to men and opinions, which modern courtesy, nay, perhaps Christian meekness would have suppressed; yet, if I mistake not, they are more sparingly employed in this, than in any contemporary controversial publication. Indeed, the higher points of what is called Calvinism, are far less insisted on, and the opponents of those points far more moderately censured than might have been expected; while the doctrines commonly called orthodox, as opposed by Pelagians, Arians, and Socinians, are strongly maintained, and the opposers of them strenuously, nay, severely, condemned. Even Mosheim allows that the triumph of the Synod was that of the Sublapsarians, not only over the Arminians, but over the Supralapsarians also.*

In order to the impartial reading of this history, it should be previously recollected, and well considered, that all the Belgic churches were, from the first, Presbyterian, in government and discipline; and constituted according to that plan, with Consistories, Classes, provincial Synods, and general Synods of all the Federated provinces; and with all those rules and methods for admission into the ministry, and to the pastoral charge in distinct congregations, as also to situations in Universities and schools of learning, which form a constituent part of it; as well as of that strict discipline, connected with it, implying not only excommunication of lay members, but the suspension or silencing of pastors; and excluding from their office, academical teachers and professors on account of heresy in doctrine, and gross inconsistency of conduct, proved

* Mosheim's Ecclesiastical History, vol. v. p. 368.

against them in their Classes, or Synods. Through the whole history, it appears, that no other form of government was proposed even by the Remonstrants, nor any thing mentioned about *toleration* in that respect; though their measures evidently tended to subvert the whole system. All the funds, likewise, reserved for religious purposes, were appropriated entirely in consistency with the Presbyterian model; and all academical honours and distinctions were conferred in that line.

This, beyond doubt, having been the case, and the principal persons concerned in the controversy against the Remonstrants, having been *zealously*, and (most of them at least) *conscientiously* attached to this system; so that it appeared to them as if the very interest of vital religion was intimately, if not inseparably, connected with it; he must, I say, be a most unreasonable and partial Anti-Presbyterian, who can expect from men of this stamp, that they would permit their whole system, and all its operations, to be retarded, disturbed, nay, totally deranged and subverted, and the whole state of their churches thrown into confusion and anarchy, without vigorous struggles to prevent a catastrophe in their view so deplorable and ruinous. Even in this age and land, few persons, of supposed candour and liberality of mind, either among zealous Episcopalians, or Independents, seem inclined tamely to witness the subversion of their favourite system, without employing the most effectual means of preventing it, which are fairly within their reach. Indeed, it is not in human nature, and cannot reasonably be expected. Nor, till men are convinced that it is not the cause of God, nor essential to that of true religion, would it be right thus to yield it up to their opponents. But when measures of this nature are adopted, at first simply in self-defence, against aggressors, in order to preserve advantages already possessed by law and custom, it must also be expected that, in the eagerness of a violent and protracted contest, even conscientious men will, through remaining prejudices and evil passions, excited and irritated by what they judge injurious usage, be betrayed into some unjustifiable measures, of which their opponents will make great advantage, and which even impartial spectators cannot justify or excuse. If, then, this should appear to have been the case in the Belgic contest, with the opposers of the Remonstrants, as well as with the Remonstrants themselves, it ought neither to excite our surprise, nor prejudice us so deeply against the whole company, as, on account of it, to involve them in one sweeping sentence of condemnation.

Again, it is well known, at least it is capable of the most complete proof, in respect of the doctrines controverted during this period in Belgium, that the Confession and Catechism of the Belgic churches were entirely on the side of the Contra-Remonstrants. Their appeal is constantly made to those articles, not under the disadvantage in which some of us in England appeal to the articles of our established church, while our opponents, with a degree of plausibility, interpret them in a different meaning, but, as to the very documents to which the Remonstrants objected, nay, which they vehemently and openly opposed, both in their sermons and public writings. So that their concessions and requisitions, in this respect, put the matter beyond all denial or doubt to him that has carefully examined the history. This will fully appear as we proceed. Now he must be a most unreasonable and unfair advocate for the Remonstrants, who would require decided and conscientious Contra-Remonstrants, holding responsible stations in the Belgic churches, universities, and schools, by virtue of their subscription to this Confession and Catechism, to suffer without any effort to the contrary, those documents to be opposed, proscribed, and vilified, and contrary doctrines promulgated, even by persons who generally held their situations in the same manner; while the opposers of the established doctrines indefatigably laboured and employed all their influence with those in authority, to set them aside and introduce the contrary doctrines; and this by the authority of the civil governments alone, to the exclusion of that ecclesiastical power, by which they in great measure had been supported. Such a passive acquiescence would not, I apprehend, be found at this day, if eager opponents should put the matter to the trial, either among decided Episcopalians, or Lutherans, or any others, who are cordially attached to their own views of Christianity. How far the defenders of the Belgic Confession and Catechism used, exclusively, "weapons of warfare not carnal, but mighty through God," is another question. It can scarcely be doubted, but there were faults on both sides, in the vehement contest, but I cannot think in an equal degree. Let the candid inquirer read and judge for himself.

In translating this history, and the other documents which I now lay before the public, I make no pretensions to any thing beyond *fairness* and *exactness*, in giving the meaning of the original. Had I been disposed to aim at it, I do not think myself competent to the office of translating in such a manner, as to invest the Latin, fairly and fully, with the entire idiom of the English language; but I have, even by design, confined myself more closely to *literal* translation, than I should have done, in an attempt less connected with controversy; and have often declined giving a more approved English word or expression, when I feared it might be suspected of not exactly conveying the sense of the original. Indeed, as far as it could be made consistent with perspicuity, I have rather *preserved* than *shunned* the Latin idiom, where any doubt could remain as to the idea which the writers intended to convey. And when, after all, I had any apprehension that I had not fully accomplished this, I have given in a parenthesis the Latin word, that the reader may judge for himself. In other places, a parenthesis often contains a word not found in the Latin, but useful in elucidating the meaning. My sole desire has been, to render the whole clearly understood by the English reader; and to call the attention of pious and reflecting persons to a part of ecclesiastical history, which I am confident has been generally less known, and more grossly misrepresented by some, and mistaken by others, than any other part whatever has been; but which, I am also persuaded, is peculiarly replete with important useful instruction, especially to zealous Calvinists, who may here learn in what a guarded, and holy, and *practical* manner, these generally *reprobated* theologians, stated and defended their tenets; and on what grounds, exclusively scriptural, they rested them.

THE HISTORY.

In the course of the last summer, the decision of the venerable Synod, lately held at Dordrecht (or Dort) concerning some heads of doctrine, which had hitherto been disputed in the Belgic churches, with the greatest disturbance of the same, was published, having been comprised in certain distinct canons. And as this most celebrated Synod had been called together, by the Illustrious and most mighty the States General, the supreme magistracy of the federated provinces, especially for the removal of the controversies, which had arisen in religion, the most of them judged that it would be sufficient, if merely the determination of the Synod concerning these same controversies were published. But when it afterwards was evident, that there were very many who greatly desired further to know, from the very acts of the Synod, what besides these things had been done in the Synod, and by what method, especially with the Remonstrant pastors: and when it was not doubtful, but that they themselves, in order to veil their own pertinacity, were about to publish some things concerning these matters, not with the best fidelity, it pleased the Illustrious and most mighty the States General, that the acts also of the same Synod, faithfully transcribed from the public registers (*tabulis*) should be published in print, for the satisfaction (*in gratiam*) and use of the churches. And as in these (records) many things every where occur, which pertain to the history of the things transacted in the Belgic churches, and which could less advantageously be understood or judged of by readers who were ignorant of these things: for which cause even the national Synod (as it may be seen in the different sessions) sometimes enjoined, especially on the deputies of the South Holland churches, to write a brief narrative of the affairs transacted with the Remonstrants: it seemed good to prefix, in the place of a preface, from it (that history) some things, which were publicly transacted; that the foreign churches especially might for once know with good fidelity what was the rise and progress of these controversies; and on what occasion, and for what causes, the illustrious and most mighty the States General convened this most celebrated Synod, at a very great expense;* especially when many things are related by the Remonstrants, in writings exhibited, and here inserted, which less accord with the truth of the things transacted.

In the Reformed churches of Federated Belgium, how great an agreement had, in the preceding age, flourished, on all the heads of orthodox doctrine, among the pastors and doctors of the Belgic churches; and moreover, how great order and decorum (εὐταξία and εὐσχημοσύνη) had al-

* "After long and tedious debates, which were frequently attended with popular tumults and civil broils, this intricate controversy was, by the counsels and authority of Maurice, prince of Orange, referred to the decision of the church, assembled in a general Synod at Dordrecht, in the year 1618." (*Mosheim*)—"It was not by the authority of prince Maurice, but by that of the States General, that the national Synod was assembled at Dordrecht. The States were not indeed unanimous; three of the seven provinces protested against the holding of this Synod, viz. Holland, Utrecht, and Overyssel." (*Maclaine.*) Mosheim's History, vol. v. p. 367.

ways been preserved in the government of the same, is too well known to the Christian world for it to be needful to set it forth in many words. This peace and harmony of the Belgic churches, lovely (in itself) and most pleasing to God and all pious men, certain persons had attempted to disturb, with unbridled violence, but not with great success: (persons) who having deserted Popery, but not being yet fully purified from its leaven, had passed over into our churches, and had been admitted into the ministry in the same, during that first scarcity of ministers: (namely) Caspius Coolhasius, of Leyden, Herman Herbertius, of Dordrecht, and Gouda, and Cornelius Wiggerus, of Horn. For in the same places, in which they had got some persons too little favouring the Reformed religion, on whose patronage they relied, this their wicked audacity was maturely repressed, as well by the authority of the supreme magistracy, as by the prudence of the pastors, and the just censures of the church; that of Coolhasius, in the national Synod at Middleburg; that of Herbertius, in the Synods of South Holland; and that of Wiggerus, in the Synods of North Holland.

Afterwards James Arminius, pastor of the most celebrated church at Amsterdam, attempted the same thing, with great boldness and enterprise; a man indeed of a more vigorous genius, (*excitatioris*,) but whom nothing pleased except that which commended itself by some show of novelty; so that he seemed to disdain most things received in the Reformed churches, even on that very account, that they had been *received*. He first paved the way for himself to this thing, by publicly and privately extenuating, and vehemently attacking (*sugillando*), the reputation and authority of the most illustrious doctors of the Reformed church, Calvin, Zanchius, Beza, Martyr, and others; that by the ruin of their name he might raise a step to glory for himself. Afterwards he began openly to propose and disseminate various heterodox opinions, nearly related to the errors of the ancient Pelagians, especially in an explanation of the epistle to the Romans; but by the vigilance and authority of the venerable Consistory of that church, his attempts were speedily opposed, lest he should be able to cause those disturbances in the church which he seemed to project (*moliri*). Yet he did not cease among his own friends, as well as among the pastors of other churches, John Utenbogardus, Adrian, Borrius, and others, whose friendship the same common studies had conciliated, to propagate his opinions, by whatever means he could; and to challenge Francis Junius, the most celebrated professor of sacred theology at Leyden, to a conference concerning the same.*

But when in the second year of this age, (Aug. 28, 1620,) that most renowned man, D. Junius, had been snatched away from the University of Leyden, with the greatest sorrow of the Belgic churches, Utenbogardus, who then favoured the opinions of Arminius, with great earnestness commended him to the most noble and ample the Curators of the University of Leyden, that he indeed might be appointed in the place of D. Junius in the professorship of sacred theology in that University. When the deputies of the churches understood this, fearing lest the vocation of a man so very much suspected of heterodoxy might sometime give cause of contentions and schism

* The lustre and authority of the college of Geneva began gradually to decline, from the time that the United Provinces, being formed into a free and independent republic, universities were founded at Leyden, Franeker and Utrecht."—Mosheim, vol. v. p, 365.

in the churches, they entreated the most noble lords, the Curators, that they would not expose the churches to those perils, but rather would think of appointing another proper person, who was free from this suspicion. And they also admonished Utenbogardus to desist from this recommendation; who, despising these admonitions, did not desist from urging his (Arminius's) vocation, until at length he had attained the same.

His vocation having been thus appointed, the Classis of Amsterdam refused to consent to his dismission; especially for this reason, because the more prudent thought that a disposition so greatly luxuriant, and prone to innovation, would be statedly employed, with more evident danger in an University, at which youth consecrated to the ministry of the churches are educated, and where greater liberty of teaching uses to be taken, than in any particular church in which it may be restrained within bounds, by the vigilance and authority of the presbytery. His dismission was notwithstanding obtained, by the frequent petitions of the lords, the Curators, of Utenbogardus, and even of Arminius himself; yet upon this condition, that a conference having been first held with Dr. Francis Gomarus, concerning the principal heads of doctrine, he should remove from himself all suspicion of heterodoxy by an explicit (*rotunda*) declaration of his opinion; when he had first promised, with a solemn attestation, that he would never disseminate his opinions, if perhaps he had any singular ones.* This conference

* How far he fulfilled this solemn promise and attestation, not only the following history, but even the histories of his most decided advocates, fully show. In fact, he fulfilled it in the very same manner that the subscriptions and most solemn engagements of numbers in our church at their ordination are fulfilled.

was held before the lords, the Curators, the deputies of the Synod also being present; in which, when he (Arminius) professed that he unreservedly (*disertè*) condemned the principal dogmas of the Pelagians concerning natural grace; the powers of free will, original sin, the perfection of man in this life, predestination, and the others; that he approved all things which Augustine and the other fathers had written against the Pelagians; and moreover that he judged the Pelagian errors had been rightly refuted and condemned by the fathers, and at the same time promised that he would teach nothing which differed from the *received doctrine* of the churches, he was admitted to the professorship of theology.*

May 6, 7, 1602.] In the beginning of this he endeavoured by every means to avert from himself every suspicion of heterodoxy; so that he defended by his support and patronage in public disputations, [October 28,] the doctrine of the Reformed churches concerning the satisfaction of Christ, justifying faith, justification by faith, the perseverance of those who truly believe, the certitude of salvation, the imperfection of man in this life, and the other heads of doctrine which he afterwards contradicted, and which, at this day, are opposed by his disciples. (This he did) contrary to his own opinion, as John Arnoldi Corvinus in a certain Dutch writing ingenuously confesses.

But when he had been now engaged in this employment as professor a year or two, it was detected that he

---

* The *received doctrine of the churches* was contained in the Belgic Confession and Catechism. Let the reader carefully attend to this, and bear it in mind while he peruses the subsequent narrative.

publicly and privately attacked (*sugillare*) most of the dogmas received in the Reformed churches, called them into doubt, and rendered them suspected to his scholars; and that he enervated the principal arguments by which they used to be maintained from the word of God, by the same exceptions, which the Jesuits, the Socinians, and other enemies of the Reformed church were accustomed to employ:* that he gave some of his own manuscript tracts privately to his scholars to be transcribed, in which he had comprised his own opinion: that he recommended in an especial manner to his scholars the writings of Castalio, Cornhertius, Suerezius, and of men like them; and that he spake contemptuously of Calvin, Beza, Martyr, Zanchius, Ursinus, and of other eminent doctors of the Reformed churches.† He moreover openly professed, that he had very many considerations or animadversions against the received doctrine which he would lay open in his own time. Some pastors, who were intimately acquainted with him, gloried that they possessed an entirely new theology. His scholars, having returned home from the University, or having been removed to other Universities, petulantly (*protervè*) insulted the

* The Reformed church included not only the church of Geneva, but the churches in Switzerland, France, Holland, England, and Scotland, and others. The doctrines opposed were then not those of Calvin or of Geneva in particular, but common to all these churches.—*T. S.*

† This is the only way in which Calvin is ever mentioned in the whole of this history, as along with many others, an eminent doctor of the Reformed churches; for it was not then supposed that there was any essential difference between the doctrine of the church at Geneva, and that of the other Reformed churches.

Reformed churches, by disputing, contradicting, and reviling their doctrine.

When the churches of Holland considered these and other things, being justly solicitous lest the purity of the Reformed doctrine having been weakened, (or *corrupted*, *labefactata*) and the youth which was educated in this seminary for the hope of the churches, imbued with depraved opinions, this matter should at length burst forth to the great mischief and disturbance of the churches: they judged that an inquiry should be thoroughly made into the whole transaction by their own deputies, to whom the common care of the churches used to be committed; so that in the next Synods it might be maturely looked to that the church might not suffer any detriment. Concerning this cause the deputies of the churches, as well of South as of North Holland, go to Arminius and state to him the rumours which were every where circulated concerning him and his doctrine, and how great solicitude possessed all the churches, and in a friendly manner they request him that if, perhaps, he found a want of any thing in the received doctrine, he would sincerely (*sincerè*, *ingenuously*) open it to his brethren, in order either that satisfaction might be given him by a friendly conference, or the whole affair might be carried before a lawful Synod. To these (persons) he answered, that he himself had never given just cause for these rumours; neither did it appear prudent in him to institute any conference with the same persons, as deputies, who would make the report concerning the matter unto the Synod; but if they would lay aside this character (*personam*) he would not decline to confer with them, as with private pastors, concerning his doctrine, on this condition, that if perhaps they should too little agree among themselves, they would report nothing of this to the Synod. As the deputies judged this to be unjust, and as the solicitude could not be taken away from the churches by a conference of this kind, they departed from him without accomplishing their purpose (*re infecta.*) Nor did they yet the less understand from the other professors of sacred theology, that various questions were eagerly agitated among the students of theology concerning predestination, free will, the perseverance of the saints, and other heads of doctrine, such as before the coming of Arminius had not been agitated among them.

July 26, 1605.] He was also admonished by the church of Leyden, of which he was a member, by the most ample and most celebrated men, Phædo Brouchovius, the consul of the city of Leyden, and Paulus Merula, professor of history (*historiarum, histories, ancient* and *modern,*) elders of the same church, that he would hold a friendly conference with his colleagues, before the Consistory of the church of Leyden, concerning those things which he disapproved in the received doctrine; from which it might be ascertained, whether, or in what dogmas, he agreed, or disagreed, with the rest of the pastors. To these (persons) he replied, that he could not do that without the leave of the Curators of the University; neither could he see what advantage would redound to the church from such a conference.

The time approached when the annual Synods of the churches in each Holland used to be held; and when, according to the custom, the grievances (*gravamina,*) of the church were sent from each of the Classes; and among the rest this also was transmitted by the Classis of Dordrecht: "Inasmuch as rumours are heard, that certain controversies concerning the doctrine of the Reformed churches have arisen in the University and church of Leyden, the Classis hath judged it to be necessary, that the Synod should deliberate on the means by which these controversies may most advantageously and speedily be settled; that all schisms, and stumbling-blocks, which might thence arise, may be removed in time, and the union of the Reformed churches be preserved against the calumnies of the adversaries." Arminius bore this very grievously, (*ægerrimè,*) and strove with all his power that this grievance should be recalled; which when he could not obtain, by the assistance of the Curators of the University, he procured a testimonial from his colleagues, in which it was declared, "That indeed more things were disputed among the students, than it was agreeable to them; but that among the professors of sacred theology themselves, as far as it appeared to them, there was no dissension in fundamentals."

A short time after the Synod of the province of South Holland was convened in the city of Rotterdam, which, when it had understood from the Classis of Dort the many and weighty reasons for which this grievance had been transmitted by the same, and at the same time, also, from the deputies of the Synod, how things really were in the University of Leyden, and what had been done by Arminius and the other professors of sacred theology; after mature deliberation, it determined that this spreading evil must be counteracted in time, neither ought the remedy of it to be procrastinated under the uncertain hope of a national Synod. And, accordingly, it enjoined on the deputies of the Synod, that they should most diligently inquire, concerning articles on which disputations were principally held among the students of theology in the University of Leyden; and should petition the lords the Curators, that a mandate might be given to the professors of sacred theology, to declare openly and explicitly their opinion concerning the same, in order that by this means it might be ascertained respecting their agreement or disagreement; and the churches, if perhaps there was no dissension, or no grievous one, might be freed from solicitude: or, if some more weighty one should be detected, they might think maturely concerning a remedy of the same.

The Synod also commanded all the pastors, for the sake of testifying their consent in doctrine, that they should subscribe the Confession and Catechism of these churches, which in many classes had been neglected, and by others refused.* The deputies of the Synod, having diligently

---

* "The opinions of Calvin, concerning *the decrees of God*, and divine grace, became daily more general, and were gradually introduced everywhere into the schools of learning. There was not, however, any public law, or *confession of faith*, that obliged the pastors of the Reformed churches in any part of the world, to conform their sentiments to the theological doctrines that were adopted and taught at Geneva."—Mosheim, vol. v. p. 366. This introduces the learned historian's account of the Synod of Dort: but the Confession and Catechism of the Belgic churches alone were appealed to in this contest, and they were certainly obligatory on all the pastors of those churches, and subscribed to by most of them. Again: "Arminius knew that the Dutch divines were neither obliged by their confession of faith, nor by any other public law, to adopt and propagate the opinions of Calvin," vol. v. p. 41. Now Arminius was not accused, as the whole history shows, of deviating from the opinions of Calvin, but for openly opposing the Confession and Catechism of the Belgic churches.

examined the matter, exhibited to the lords, the curators, nine questions concerning which they had understood, that at this time disputations were principally maintained, and they requested that it might be enjoined by their authority on the professors of sacred theology, to explain fully their opinion concerning the same. But they answered, that some hope now shone forth of obtaining a national Synod in a short time; and therefore they judged it more prudent (*consultius*) to reserve these questions to the same, than by any further inquisition respecting them to give a handle to dissension. The pastors also, who had embraced the opinion of Arminius, everywhere in the Classes refused to obey the mandate of the Synod, concerning the subscription of the Confession and the Catechism.

This matter increased the solicitude of the churches, when they saw that these pastors, relying on the favour of certain persons, evidently despised the authority of the Synod, and more boldly (*audaciùs*) persisted in their attempt. Wherefore, as in that way a remedy could not be applied to this evil, they copiously explained to the most illustrious and mighty lords, the States General, in how great a danger the church was placed; and petitioned, that in order to the taking away of these evils, a national Synod, which had now been for many years deferred, might be called together by the authority of the same persons, at the earliest opportunity. These (the States General) declared, that the states of all the provinces had already agreed on the convocation of a national Synod; but that there were those among them, who, in the letters of consent, had added this condition, or, as they called it, *clause:* Namely, that in the same there should be a revision of the Confession and Catechism of these churches, and, consequently, the convocation of a national Synod could not be made, unless this clause were added, without the detriment (*prœjudicio*) of the States of that province. But as it was not obscurely evident, who for some years had counselled (*authores fuissent*) the illustrious the States of Holland, that this clause should be added, and even pressed; and as it might be feared, if it should be annexed to the calling of the Synod, that they who earnestly desired changes of doctrine, would abuse the same; and at the same time also, lest (especially in this state of things) it should afford no light cause of offence to the churches; as if the illustrious States themselves, or our churches, doubted of the truth of the doctrine comprised in this Confession and Catechism; the deputies of the churches petition that the convocation of the Synod should be drawn up in general terms, as they call them, in the manner hitherto customary; especially as this clause seemed the less necessary, seeing that in national Synods it had always been permitted, if any one thought that he had ought against any article of these writings, fairly and duly to propose it.

But the illustrious lords, the States General, declared, that this clause was not so to be understood, as if they desired any thing to be changed by it, in the doctrine of these churches; for indeed a doctrine was not always changed by a revisal (or recognition, *recognitione*,) but sometimes was even confirmed; yet it could not be omitted without the prejudice of that province, which had expressly added it. They therefore delivered the letters of consent, in which this also had been added, to the deputies of the churches, which they transmitted to the churches of each of the provinces; and with them they also signified what pains they had bestowed that it might be omitted.

March 15, 1606.] The Belgic churches, on the receipt of these letters, rejoiced indeed that, after the expectation of so many years, at length the power of holding a national Synod had been obtained, though they were not a little stumbled by this clause. Not because they were unwilling that the Confession and the Catechism should be recognized, after the accustomed and due manner, in the national Synod; but because they feared lest they, who were labouring for a change of doctrine, should be rendered more daring, as if by this clause a power was granted to them by the public authority of the lords, the States, of moving and innovating whatever any one pleased; and that these discords and controversies had arisen from them, not from the inordinate desire of innovating, but from an earnest endeavour to satisfy the decrees of the illustrious, the States. In the same letters the illustrious lords, the States General, gave information that it had been determined by them to call together some learned and peaceful theologians from each of the provinces, that they might deliberate with the same, concerning the time, place, and manner of holding this national Synod.

August, 1606.] While these things were transacting, the annual Synod of the churches of Holland was held at Groningen; in which, when the deputies of the churches had related what had been done by them in the cause of the national Synod, and what had been determined by the illustrious lords, the States General, it was judged proper to enjoin on the same (deputies) diligently to press the convocation of a national Synod; and though the Synod thought that the Confession and Catechism would be recognized, in a way and manner new and unaccustomed hitherto, in the national Synod, it purposed that those persons who should be called together by the States of Holland, out of South Holland, to the convention, in which (it was to be deliberated) concerning the time, place and manner of holding the national Synod, should be admonished to petition from the States General, in the name of these churches, that the clause, of which it hath before been spoken, might be omitted in the letters of convocation, for the reasons before assigned; and that, in the place of it, other milder words, which might produce less offence, might be substituted.

It was also enjoined in the same Synod, to all the pastors of the churches of South Holland, and to all the professors of sacred theology in the University of Leyden, that, at as early a time as could be, they should exhibit the considerations or animadversions, which they had upon the doctrine contained in the Confession and Catechism; (because Arminius and the pastors who were attached to him were often accustomed to glory that they had very many;) the pastors indeed in their own Classes, but the professors to the deputies of the churches; that the same might be lawfully carried unto the national Synod, if satisfaction could not be given to them in the Classes. When this was demanded of the pastors attached to Arminius, they declined proposing them in the Classes, because, they said, they were not yet prepared, but that they would propose them in their own time and manner. Arminius also having been admonished concerning this thing by the deputies of the churches, answered that it could not be done at that time with edification; but that, in the national Synod, he would fully lay open the same.

May 23, 1607.] And when, not long after, the illustrious, the States General, called together some theologians out of each of the provinces, with whom they might deliberate respecting the time, place, and manner of the national Synod, namely, John Leo and John Fontanus, from Gueldria; Francis Gomarus, James Arminius, John Utenbogardus, and John Becius, out of South Holland; Herman Frankelius and Henry Brandius, out of Zealand; Everard Botius and Henry Johannis, out of the province of Utrecht; Sibrander Lubertus and Jannes Bogermannus, out of Friesland; Thomas Goswinius, out of Transisulania; John Acronus and John Nicasias, out of the city Groningen and Omland; the questions, concerning which it should be deliberated in this convention, were proposed to them by the illustrious, the States General; and it was declared by their concurrent suffrages, that as to the time it was necessary that the Synod should be called together as soon as might be in the beginning of the ensuing summer. [A. D. 1608.] That, as to place, the city of Utrecht would be the most convenient for holding the Synod: as to the manner, 1. That the grievances to be discussed in the Synod should be brought before the national Synod from each of the provincial Synods. 2. That from each of the several Synods, and by the suffrages of the same, four pastors and two elders should be deputed; in the place of which elders also, men of singular condition, and skill in matters of theology, and adorned by a testimony of piety, though they did not fill up any ecclesiastical office, might be deputed. 3. That to these deputies power should be given in all things which should be treated of in the Synod, not of deliberating only, but also of determining and deciding. 4. That the rule of judgment in all the controversies relating to doctrines and morals should be the written word of God, or the sacred Scriptures alone.* 5. That to the national Synod should be called together, not only the churches which are in Federated Belgium, namely, of each language, the Dutch and French, but those also of the Belgic nation which are dispersed without Belgium, whether they were collected under the cross, or otherwise (*alibi*). 6. That the illustrious and most mighty, the States General, should be requested that they would deign to send to the same their own delegates professing the Reformed religion, that, in their name, they might preside over the order of it. 7. That the professors also of sacred theology should be called to the same.

In these things indeed they were all agreed, as in some others they could not agree among themselves. For

* This rule completely excluded all human reasoning, authority, tradition, or new revelations, as opposed to the written word, "the sure testimony" of God; not only the authority of fathers and councils, with the traditions of the church of Rome, but the authority also of the church of Geneva, of Calvin, and of all other Reformed teachers. How is it then that ecclesiastical historians generally represent this contest as an attempt to impose the doctrine of the church of Geneva on the Belgic churches? It might as reasonably be said that the clergymen and others who combined and used every effort, some years since, to procure the abolishment of subscription to the articles of the church of England, but could not succeed, had the doctrines of Calvin and Geneva imposed on them. Whatever similarity there might be between the doctrine of Calvin, or that of the church of Geneva, and the Confession and Catechism of the Belgic churches, the latter was exclusively appealed to by the other pastors, and avowedly opposed by Arminius and his followers; yet even these were to be revised according to the written word of God.

Arminius and Utenbogardus, and the two (deputies) from Utrecht, whom they had drawn over to their opinion, determined these three things: 1. That that was to be held as the decision of the Synod, not which had been determined by the votes of all the deputies to the Synod, but also by those who deputed them; for, under the name of the Synod, not the deputies alone, but those who deputed them also, ought to be understood. 2. That it should always be free to the deputies, as often as they might choose, and as they perceived that they were burdened in any thing, to retire to their own (friends or constituents) for the sake of taking counsel. 3. That the revision of the Belgic Confession and Catechism was altogether necessary; so that they saw no cause, for which the clause concerning the revision of those writings, should not be inserted in the letters of convocation.

The rest of the pastors and professors judged: 1. That that should be considered as the definite decision of the Synod, which had been determined either by the concurrent votes of the deputies to the Synod, or of the majority of them; but that, under the name of the Synod, those were to be accounted, who, as lawful deputies to the same, had met together with the power of judging. 2. That it might indeed be allowed them to retire to their friends for the sake of taking counsel; yet so that, under this pretext, the proceedings of the Synod should not be rashly disturbed: that when, and in what manner, and for what causes, they might thus recede, should not be left to the unrestricted will (*arbitrio*) of individuals, but to the judgment of the whole Synod. 3. That the Belgic Confession and Catechism might indeed be revised in the Synod, if, for adequate causes, the Synod should determine that this was necessary; and likewise that it should be free to all, who thought that they had any thing against those writings, to propose the same to the Synod in due manner, to be examined and decided on; but because the clause concerning the revision, if it should be inserted in the letters of convocation, seemed likely to give to some cause of offence, and to others the license of innovating; they thought that the illustrious, the States General, should be petitioned that this clause, for the sake of the tranquillity of the churches, might be omitted in the letters of convocation; and that, in the place of it, these, or similar words, might be substituted, namely, That the Synod was convened for the confirmation, agreement, and propagation of pure and orthodox doctrine; for preserving and establishing the peace and good order (εὐταξίαν) of the church; and finally, for promoting true piety among the inhabitants of these regions. And most of them showed that they had this very thing in the mandates from their own churches, and also from the States themselves of their own provinces. This disagreement of counsels and judgments threw in a new delay to the national Synod; for they who had hitherto resisted its convocation, eagerly seizing on this occasion, laboured earnestly by all means, that the convocation of the Synod, though now promised, might be hindered.

In this convention Arminius was requested, with the strongest obtestation, by the other professors and pastors, that the things which he had (to allege) against the doctrine expressed in the Confession and Catechism, he would, in a free and brotherly manner, communicate to them as his fellow ministers; the promise being added, that they would bestow pains fully to satisfy him, or that he, on honourable conditions, might be reconciled to his colleagues, and might thenceforth live peaceably with them; neither would they, a reconciliation having been effected, publish beyond the place of the convention any of those things which he should make manifest unto them. But he said, that neither was this thought prudent by him, nor was he bound to do it, as the convention was not appointed for this purpose. In the following summer, when the annual Synod of the South Holland churches was held at Delft, Utenbogardus was admonished to explain to the Synod the reasons on account of which, in giving the counsels concerning the manner of holding the national Synod, he, with Arminius, had thought and advised differently from the rest of the pastors, that the same might be well considered and decided on by the Synod. He answered that he was bound to render an account of this to the illustrious, the States alone, and not to the Synod. Being requested that he would explain those things which he had (to allege) against the doctrine that was contained in the Confession and Catechism of these churches, he replied, that neither did it appear to him prudent to do it in that assembly, nor was he prepared. It was in this Synod also inquired, whether, according to the decree of the former Synod, any considerations, or animadversions, upon the Confession and Catechism had been exhibited to the Classes; but it was answered by the delegates from each of the Classes, that most of the pastors had professed in the Classes that they had no animadversions against the received doctrine, but that those who professed that they had some were unwilling to explain them, either because they said that they were not yet prepared, or because they did not think that this was advisable for them.* Wherefore the Synod judged that it should again be enjoined on them, that, omitting all evasions, subterfuges, (*tergiversationibus,*) and delays, they should explain, as early as might be, all the animadversions which they had against the received doctrine; each of them to his own Classis.

It was likewise shown to the Synod, that every where in the churches dissensions daily more and more increased; and that most of the young men coming forth from the University of Leyden, and the instruction of Arminius, being called to the ministry of the churches, in the examination indeed concealed their opinion by ambiguous methods of speaking; but when they had been set forth to the ministry, they immediately moved new disputations, contended earnestly for opinions, and gloried that they had various considerations against the received doctrine; that in the Classes and Consistories, sharp dissensions and altercations arose among the pastors, concerning most of the heads of doctrine; and that among the people also, various disputings concerning doctrine were heard, with the great offence and disturbance of the churches; yea, moreover, that the beginnings of schisms were seen; that the pastors attached to Arminius instituted frequent meetings, in which they might de-

---

* Nothing can be more evident than this fact, that the followers of Arminius aimed to subvert, or exceedingly to modify, the doctrine of the authorized writings of the Belgic churches; and that the others wanted no alteration to be made in that doctrine, as more favourable, either to the doctrine of the church of Geneva, or of Calvin, as many writers confidently assert.

liberate concerning the propagation of their doctrine; and that the people more and more went away into parties.*

As therefore the Synod judged that the remedy of this evil could no longer be deferred, and that the hope of obtaining a national Synod, because of this diversity of counsels and opinions, was altogether uncertain: it was determined by the Synod, from the counsel of the most ample the delegates, to petition of the illustrious lords, the States of Holland and West Friesland, that from the two Synods of South and North Holland, one provincial Synod might be called at the first opportunity, (as it had formerly been done in similar difficulties,) in order to quiet and remove these evils. When the deputies of each Synod had copiously explained to the illustrious lords, the States, these difficulties of the churches, as growing more and more heavy; and had petitioned, that for the removal of the same the convocation of a provincial Synod might be appointed at the most early time: though great hopes had been given them, by the most ample the lords the delegates, they were not as yet able to obtain it; because at that time, [Sept. 14, 1607,] a beginning had been

* The enlightened and decided friend to free inquiry, will see, even in the causes of these complaints, (while the *immediate* effects may perhaps be deemed very unfavourable to truth and holiness,) the dawn of that more enlarged state of things, in which free investigation of both received and exploded, and of novel opinions, proves ultimately and highly beneficial to the cause of truth: and he will agree, that the arm of authority, secular or ecclesiastical, could not beneficially be exerted against it; except so far as to require those who voluntarily belong to, and minister in any church, to conform to the rules of that church, or to recede from it without further molestation. But this does not prevent the propriety of doing justice to the character of wise and pious men, to whom no views of this kind had as yet ever been presented.

made of settling the terms of a truce with the enemy; and the illustrious States being themselves fully occupied with the most weighty affairs of the republic, could not have leisure to attend to these ecclesiastical concerns.

April 30, 1608.] In the mean time Arminius, when he saw that the churches were urgent that this cause should be determined by the legal ecclesiastical judgments, in order that he might decline that trial, (*forum*, meaning the decision of the ecclesiastical courts,) having exhibited a suppliant writing (*libellum*), to the illustrious, the States, obtained that cognizance should be taken of his cause, by the most ample the counsellors of the supreme court, being *political* men (not *ecclesiastical*); and Gomarus was commanded to hold a conference with Arminius before the same, the pastors being present, who had lately attended at the preparatory convention from South and North Holland. When the deputies of the churches had understood this, they again requested the illustrious, the States of Holland and West Friesland, that instead of this conference instituted before the supreme court, a provincial Synod might be called; that in the same, cognizance might be taken and judgment given on this ecclesiastical cause, by ecclesiastical men, skilful in these matters, and lawfully delegated by the churches, with the power of awarding judgment. The illustrious, the States, answered, that the cognizance of the cause alone had been entrusted to the supreme court; but that the *decision* of it would afterwards be committed, either to a provincial or to a national Synod.

In this conference a long dispute occurred about the order of proceeding. Arminius contended that Gomarus ought to undertake the part of an *agent*, (*actoris*, pleader, or prosecutor, or accuser,) but that he was only bound to defend himself; while Gomarus judged, that this method of proceeding was not less unjust than unusual, especially in an ecclesiastical cause, before political judges; that he indeed was prepared to bring proof before a lawful Synod that Arminius had proposed dogmas which were at variance with the word of God, and with the Confession and Catechism of the Belgic churches; but that it could not be done in this place, without prejudice to his cause; that he, (Gomarus,) thought this conference, in order to answer the intention of the illustrious lords, the States, might better be conducted in this manner, namely, that without these mutual accusations, each of them should clearly and perspicuously explain and set forth his own opinion, concerning every one of the heads of doctrine; for thence it might most advantageously be understood in what things they agreed or disagreed. As to what belonged to himself, he would not shrink from explaining his opinion concerning all the heads of doctrine, fully and openly, as much so, indeed, as could be desired by any one; that Arminius also, if he were willing fully to perform the part of a faithful teacher, ought in the same manner to declare his own opinion, and not any longer in this business to use subterfuges of this kind. He (Arminius) nevertheless persisted in his purpose; so that he at length exclaimed that he wondered, seeing various rumours of his heretodoxy had gone about through the churches, and the conflagration excited by him was said to rise above the very roofs of the churches, that he yet found no one who dared to lodge an accusation against him. Gomarus, in order to meet this boasting, undertook to prove that he had taught such an opinion concerning the first article of our faith, namely, concerning the justification of man before God, as was opposed to the word of God, and to the Confession of the Belgic churches. For the proof of this thing, he produced his own very words, written out from the hand-writing of the same Arminius, in which he asserts, that in the justification of man before God, the righteousness of Christ is not imputed for righteousness; but that faith itself, or the act of believing (το *credere*), by the gracious acceptation (*acceptationem, acquittal*), was that our righteousness by which we are justified before God. When Arminius saw himself thus fast bound, as he could not indeed deny this to be evidence of proof, (*evidentiam probationis, conclusive evidence,*) he began to consent to another method of proceeding, namely, that each should sign in a writing his own opinion comprised in certain theses, concerning the principal articles in which the difference was thought to consist; on which each afterwards, in return, marked his own animadversions.

This conference having been terminated, the counsellors of the supreme court reported to the illustrious, the States of Holland and West Friesland, that they, as far as they had been able to perceive from the conference, judged that the controversies which had arisen between these two professors, were not of so great importance, but regarded especially some more subtile disputes concerning Predestination, which might either be omitted or connived at, (*dissimulari,*) by a mutual toleration. But Gomarus added, that the difference detected in the opinions were of so great moment, that he, with the opinion of Arminius, should not dare to appear before the judgment of God: and unless a remedy were maturely applied, it was to be feared lest, in a short time, one province should be engaged in contest against another, church against church, state against state, and citizens against each other. But the illustrious, the States, determined that the writings sealed on each side in this conference should be preserved in the supreme court, even unto a national Synod, neither should they be communicated in the meanwhile to any man (*cuiquam mortalium*). Yet neither did this conference deliver from anxiety the churches, but rather increased it; especially as the things which had been done at it were concealed from the churches. For not without reason (*haud temere*), they judged that this was done in favour of Arminius, lest his opinions should be made manifest. In the meanwhile the churches did not cease, by their deputies, strenuously to petition the illustrious States, that this ecclesiastical cause, which, except with great danger of the church, could not be deferred, might be examined and decided on, as soon as possible, by the judgment either of a lawful provincial, or a national Synod. When Arminius understood this, he procured by Utenbogardus, whose authority at that time was great among most of the chief persons of the country, that the illustrious States should command, that the annual Synods themselves, as well of South as of North Holland, the time of which was at hand, should be deferred. But as this could not be done without the greatest detriment of the churches, they again, having explained before the illustrious, the States, their difficulties, petitioned, either that it might be allowed to hold, according to custom, each of the annual Synods, as well that in South as in North Holland; or that out of each united together one provincial Synod should as soon as possible be called, as it had also before this been petitioned.

June 28, 1608.] To this petition, the illustrious States declared, that they had determined, in the next October, to call together a provincial Synod for this purpose. When this had been made known to the churches, all the pastors attached to Arminius were again admonished, that each of them should lay open to his Classis his considerations, (or remarks, *considerationes*,) that the same might be lawfully carried to the approaching Synod. But they, as before, so now also each of them, declined this with one consent, with their accustomed evasions (*tergiversationibus*). And when the month of October approached, and the churches pressed the convocation of a provincial Synod, as promised, that was again deferred for two months: and it was again permitted to the churches, to hold the particular annual Synods, as well in South as in North Holland; yet on this condition, that the cause of Arminius should not be treated of in the same, which they willed to be reserved to the provincial Synod. In the Synod of the churches of South Holland, which was held at Dordrecht (or Dort), when it had been reported that all the pastors attached to Arminius were hitherto unwilling to lay open their considerations, which they said they had against the received doctrine, to their fellow pastors (*symmistis*), but that they eluded by various evasions the admonitions of the churches and the decrees of the Synods, it was determined that it should be gravely enjoined on them, to lay open these their considerations within the space of the next month, after the admonition given, under the penalty of incurring the ecclesiastical censure against the contumacious. The same also was demanded from the professors of sacred theology in the University of Leyden, and from Peter Bertius, the ruler of the theological college. These pastors, when they saw that either their opinion must be laid open, or they must undergo the ecclesiastical censure; in order to evade each of these, they, by the aid of Utenbogardus, obtained letters from the illustrious lords, the States, in which it was enjoined on these pastors, that within the space of one month they should transmit to the lords, the States themselves, the considerations which they had sealed up, that they might be reserved by the same, to be exhibited to the provincial Synod. The professors being asked by the deputies of the Synod, if they had any considerations of this kind, to open these before them, Gomarus answered, indeed, that he had observed nothing in the Confession and Catechism of the churches which he thought in need of correction or alteration, as too little agreeing with the word of God; but Arminius, that he would answer by writing to this demand, in his own time. And when he saw himself thus urged by the churches to the declaration of his opinion, he explained in a prolix discourse to the lords, the States, in their stated convention, what he thought concerning divine predestination, the grace of God, and the free-will of man, the perseverance of the saints, the assurance of salvation, the perfection of man in this life, the deity of the Son of God, the justification of man before God, and the other heads of doctrine. At the same time, he endeavoured to persuade the illustrious, the States, that in these Reformed churches, a doctrine was delivered concerning the divine predestination, which was at variance (*pugnaret*) with the nature of God, with his wisdom, justice, and goodness; with the nature of man and his free-will; with the work of the creation; with the nature of life and death eternal, and finally with that of sin; and which took away the divine grace, was inimical to the glory of God, and pernicious to the salvation of men; which made God the author of sin, hindered sorrow for sin, took away all pious solicitude, lessened the earnest desire of doing good things, extinguished the ardour of prayer, took away the "fear and trembling," with which we ought to "work out our own salvation," made way for desperation, subverted the gospel, hindered the ministry of the word, and lastly, overturned the foundations, not only of the Christian religion, but also wholly of all religion.*

When Gomarus had heard these things, he deemed it a part of his duty, to give better information (*meliùs erudire*) to the illustrious lords, the States, lest perhaps

* It is probable that in all the volumes which ever since that time have been written by Arminians, or Anti-Calvinists, in refutation of Calvinism, there is no objection of any plausibility urged against the doctrines designated by that term, which is not here briefly, and fairly, and emphatically stated, as used by Arminius, before the States of Holland, in this history, written with the express purpose of sanctioning the decisions of the Synod of Dort: perhaps no where else can so compendious a list of these objections be found. The compilers evidently did not consider them as unanswerable, or very formidable; nor were they afraid of having the whole cause fairly tried and determined according to THE WORD OF GOD; the objections being, indeed, neither more nor less than man's presumptuous reasonings against the express, sure, and authoritative testimony of God himself; the substance of the inquiry which the apostle answered, or silenced at once, "Thou wilt say to me, Why doth he yet find fault? For who hath resisted his will? Nay but, O man," rejoins the apostle, "who art thou that repliest against God?" It is evident from the whole narrative, that the Confession and Catechism of the Belgic churches, as well as the sermons and writings of the pastors, were involved in this heavy charge, and condemned most deeply by this sweeping sentence.

by this method, their minds should be pre-occupied with unfavourable prejudices against the orthodox doctrine. Having therefore petitioned for permission to speak, he, in the same convention, copiously (*prolixè*) explained what was the genuine opinion of Arminius concerning the grace of God, and the free will of man, the justification of man before God, the perfection of man in this life, predestination, the origin of sin, and the perseverance of the saints; and what just cause of suspicion he (Arminius) had given, that he did not think aright, concerning the Holy Scripture, the sacred Trinity, the providence of God, the satisfaction of Jesus Christ, the church, faith, good works, and the other heads of doctrine. By what arts also he disseminated his own opinions; namely, that when publicly asked and solemnly enjoined, he has hitherto concealed his opinion from the churches; but had diligently inculcated it privately on the pastors, whom he hoped he should be able to draw over into it, and on his own pupils (or scholars); that he enervated the principal arguments of our party, (*nostrorum*) with which the orthodox doctrine used to be fortified; but confirmed those of the Jesuits, and of the other adversaries, with which they are accustomed to fight against the doctrine of the Reformed churches; that he suggested various doubts concerning the truth of the received doctrine, into the minds of the pupils; and (taught them) to hold the same at first as in an equilibrium with the heterodox doctrine, and at length altogether to reject it; that hitherto he had not been willing to publish any declaration of sincerity and consent in doctrine, though very often lovingly, and in a brotherly manner, asked by the churches to do it; that he had earnestly laboured by all means, that he might not lay open to the churches his errors, which had been detected before the supreme court; and that he had aimed at this one thing, by delaying the time, to have the opportunity of drawing over the more persons into his own opinion, and of every where occupying the churches; that, having despised the decisions and decrees of Synods, Classes, and Consistories, he had in the first instance burst forth (*prosiliisse*) to the tribunal of the Supreme Magistrate, and had there proposed his complaints and accusations against the doctrine of the churches; and by the arts of a courtier (*aulicas*) had industriously studied to conciliate favour to himself, but to bring hatred on the churches. Wherefore he (Gomarus) earnestly entreated the States, (seeing that the students of sacred theology in the University of Leyden, and every where the pastors daily more and more revolted from the orthodox doctrine; discords and contentions spread abroad; the churches were disturbed, and the citizens were drawn into parties,) that the promised national Synod might as early as possible be called, in which the causes of these evils having been legally examined, a suitable remedy might at length be applied. The deputies of the churches also soon after petitioned for the same; but by the endeavours of Utenbogardus and others it was effected, that this calling of the Synod should always be deferred.

April 4, 1609.] They (the deputies of the churches) likewise several times admonished Arminius, to send to them the considerations contained in the writing which he had promised, who at length answered by letter, that he did not deny that this had been promised by him, but because he had understood that the illustrious, the States,

9

had ordered the pastors to send their considerations sealed up unto them, he had changed his mind (*consilium*), and that he would wait till the same also should be enjoined on him. Peter Bertius, the regent of the theological college, being admonished by the same deputies that if he had anything against the received doctrine of the churches he would freely explain it, declared his own opinion concerning most of the heads of doctrine openly, without any evasion, and showed that, in the articles of the justification of man before God, of predestination, of the grace of God, of free-will, and finally, of the perseverance of true believers (*verè fidelium*), he thought differently from the doctrine of the Belgic churches.* This rendered the churches more and more anxious, seeing they understood that not only Arminius in the University, but Bertius also, in the seminary of the churches of Holland, set before the youth entrusted to his fidelity, and destined to the ministry of the churches, heterodox doctrine; and having drawn them aside from the sincerity (or *purity*) of the doctrine, instilled into them (*imbuere*) new opinions. The churches saw these things, and grieved; yet they were

* "There was not, however, any public law, or *confession of faith*, that obliged the pastors of the Reformed churches in any part of the world, to conform their sentiments to the theological doctrines that were adopted and taught at Geneva." Mosheim, vol. v. p. 366. "Arminius knew that the Dutch divines and doctors were not obliged by their confession of faith, nor by any public law, to adopt and propagate the principles of Calvin." Ibid. p. 441. It might be supposed from this, that the opposers of Arminius, and all concerned in procuring the Synod of Dort, wanted Arminius and his party to adhere to the Geneva Confession and the creed of Calvin, &c.: whereas, in fact, these are never mentioned in the history prefixed to that of the Synod, but the received doctrine of the Belgic churches alone.

not able to apply the lawful remedy to these evils, though it was that which they chiefly wished and judged necessary; Utenbogardus, and others, whose authority was at that time great among certain chief persons of the country, hindering with all their power, by their means, all synodical conventions and ecclesiastical judgments.

Hence the pastors attached to Arminius were made more bold to propose their own heterodox opinions; and they began even publicly before the people to defame the received doctrine with various calumnies, and to rage furiously (*debacchari*) against it, as horrid and detestable. Among these, a certain person, (called) Adolphus Venator, the pastor of the church of Alcmar in North Holland, was not the last; who, besides that he was of too little approved a life, (*vitæ minùs probatæ,*) openly and by no means in a dissembling manner, scattered abroad Pelagian and Socinian errors, with incredible impudence, publicly and privately; for which cause he was suspended from the office of teaching, by the legitimate judgment of the churches of North Holland. He (however) despising the judgment of the churches, persisted in the office of teaching, against the will of the churches. The orthodox pastors in the Classis of Alcmar judged that this unholy man (*impurum*), having been lawfully suspended from the ministry, and a few other pastors whom he had drawn over into his opinion, and who pertinaciously refused to testify their consent to the doctrine of the Reformed churches, by the subscription of the Confession, should not be admitted into their assembly. They, having complained of this matter to the illustrious, the States, by the aid of Utenbogardus, obtained a mandate, by which this admission for them was commanded; which, when the orthodox could not do, because of their conscience, they submissively requested the illustrious, the States, that they might not be burdened by mandates of this kind, which they could not conscientiously obey. The deputies of the churches, when they saw that these dissensions and scandals were daily more and more increased, again earnestly entreated (or adjured, *obtestati sunt*) the illustrious, the States, in the name of the churches, that the promised provincial Synod might be called together at the earliest time, for the removal of these evils. But when Utenbogardus, and the rest of the pastors addicted to Arminius, observed the minds of the illustrious lords, the States, to incline to this, in order that they might avoid the ecclesiastical decisions, they effected, by certain individuals who seemed more attached to their cause, that in the stead of the provincial Synod, a conference, concerning the controverted articles between Gomarus and Arminius, should be held, in the convention itself, of the illustrious States; in the which each might take to himself four pastors, whose counsels they might be allowed to use. Arminius had taken Jannes Utenbogardus, of Hague, Adrian Borrius of Leyden, Nicholas Grevinchovius of Rotterdam, and the before mentioned Adolphus Venator of the Alcmarian church. But Gomarus (took) Ricardus Acronius of Scheidam, James Roland of Amsterdam, John Bogardus of Harlem, and Festus Hommius of Leyden, pastors of the church.

When they had come together, Gomarus and the pastors, who had joined themselves to him, requested these two things: 1. That this conference should be instituted in writing, to be exhibited on each side; by which means, vain rumours of whatever kind might be counteracted.

2. That these writings should afterwards be delivered to a national Synod, to be examined and judged, by which the judgment of an ecclesiastical cause might be reserved entire to the churches.* The illustrious, the States, willed that the conference should be instituted, by word of mouth, (*vivâ voce*,) yet so that it might be allowed to use writing in aid of the memory; and they promised, having given public letters for confirmation of the matter, that this cause, when they had known concerning the same from this conference, should be reserved to the judgment of a provincial Synod; and in order to this, that all things whatever, which should there be treated of by word of mouth, being afterwards sealed up in writing, those writings should be exhibited to the Synod.

The same persons also thought it a shameful thing, (*indignum*,) that Adolphus Venator, who, on account of his doctrine and impure life, had been suspended from the ministry by the lawful censures of the churches, should be brought forward (or employed, *adhiberi*) in such a conference, to the great detriment of ecclesiastical censures. Wherefore they demanded, that another person should be taken in his place; which, as Arminius vehemently struggled against it, they were not able to obtain. In the beginning also, a disputation occurred concerning

* That this cause might be regularly condemned, it was judged "proper to bring it before an ecclesiastical assembly or Synod. This method of proceeding was agreeable to the sentiments and principles of the Calvinists, who are of opinion, that all spiritual concerns and religious controversies ought to be judged and decided by an ecclesiastical assembly or council."—*Mosheim*, vol. v. p. 450. "The Calvinists are not particular in this; and indeed it is natural that debates, purely theological, should be discussed in an assembly of divines."—*Note, Ibid. Maclaine.*

the order of handling the articles. For Arminius seemed to place the great defence of his cause in this, that the beginning should be made with the article of predestination. Gomarus thought, that because the article which respected justification seemed more necessary, the beginnings should be made with it; which also pleased the illustrious, the States.*

Concerning this article, there was the same controversy, which had previously been agitated before the supreme court, namely, whether faith, inasmuch as it is an *act* according to the gracious estimation of God, be that righteousness itself by which we are justified before God. In the second place, it was treated concerning the doctrine of divine predestination, which Arminius endeavoured to render odious by the same consequences, which he had lately brought forward in the convention of the illustrious, the States. But Gomarus urged the principal point, namely, Whether faith were the *antecedent cause* or *condition* of election, or whether indeed the *fruit* or *effect* of the same. The third controversy was concerning the grace of God and free-will. Arminius professed that he acknowledged all the operations of divine grace, whatever could be assigned in the conversion of man; only that no grace should be assigned, which is *irresistible*. Gomarus showed what ambiguity and what guile might be concealed under that word *irresistible;* namely,

* Arminius on this point showed his sound policy; for when declamations against predestination have prepared the way, a prejudice as to the other doctrines connected with it, or held by those who hold that offensive doctrine, will seldom be impartially considered. Some modern refuters of Calvinism either have not been so *politic,* or they have been *more fair,* in this respect, than Arminius was.

that indeed under the same might be hidden the doctrine of the Semi-Pelagians, and the Synergists (Co-operators), which had been condemned of old: and he stated, that in the regeneration of man, that grace of the Holy Spirit was necessary, which works so efficaciously, that the resistance of the flesh being overcome, whosoever are made partakers of this grace, are certainly and infallibly converted to God by the same. Finally, they treated concerning the perseverance of the truly believing. Arminius declared, that he had never opposed the doctrine of the certain perseverance of the truly believing, nor thus far was he willing to oppose it, because those testimonies of Scripture stood for it (or were extant for it) to which he was not as yet able to answer; he should therefore only propose those topics, which, in this article, had excited scruple and hesitation in him.* When Gomarus had answered to these topics, he confirmed this doctrine from the word of God by many evident testimonies.

These things having been fully discussed, the collocutors were asked whether there remained more articles, concerning which they differed from each other. Gomarus answered, that there were more: the articles, for instance, concerning original sin, the providence of God, the authority of the sacred scriptures, the assurance of salva-

* It is remarkable, that Arminius himself in this his last public conference, and just before his death, should express himself so undecided on this grand point of decided and unqualified opposition to modern Arminians; and should make the concession, that he was not yet able to answer the Scriptures, which seemed to favour the doctrine of the final perseverance of all true believers. It is worthy the serious consideration of his disciples. He died Oct. 10, in this same year.

tion, the perfection of man in this life, and some others, concerning which, whether they should treat also in this place, he left to the prudence of the illustrious, the States; especially as they must a second time be discussed by them in the Synod. But when the state of Arminius's health did not seem such as could endure a longer conference, it pleased the illustrious, the States, that it should be broken off; after that, they had promised to the petition of Gomarus and the rest of the pastors, who had joined themselves to him, that this entire cause should be more fully examined and decided on in a provincial Synod, to be called together as soon as might be; and had enjoined the collocutors, that each of them should exhibit to them his opinion with the arguments and refutations of the contrary opinion, contained in a writing, within the space of fourteen days, in order that these writings might be preserved by them, even to the provincial Synod. Gomarus within the prescribed time transmitted his writings, which were afterwards published in Dutch (*Belgicè*).

As the difficulties of the church were rather increased than taken away by this conference, the deputies of the churches submissively again petitioned the illustrious, the States, that the provincial Synod, so often before, and in the conference itself promised, should be called, and also at the earliest time. Answer was returnêd to them, though there were certain persons who strove against it, that the convocation of it would then be appointed, when the pastors of the Alcmarian Classis had obeyed the mandate of the illustrious, the States, admitting to their assembly Adolphus Venator, and the pastors attached to him. But lest that affair should delay the provincial Synod, the deputies of the churches going to Alcmar treated with the pastors of that Classis concerning this admission, and so far prevailed on them that they were ready to admit the pastors attached to Venator, on honourable conditions (or equitable, *honestis*); but they laid before the deputies so many and weighty reasons why they could not admit Venator himself, that they themselves judged that, in this respect, they ought not to be urged. When this had been reported to the illustrious, the States, not even yet could the calling of a Synod be obtained. For indeed the pastors attached to Arminius effected this, that it should be again enjoined to the Classis of Alcmar, unreservedly to admit these pastors without any condition; which when they could not do, the calling (*of the Synod*) was again hindered.*

Arminius in the meanwhile excused himself to the illustrious States by letters; that by reason of bodily weakness he was not able to prepare the writing enjoined him;

* "These measures confirmed instead of removing the apprehensions of the Calvinists; from day to day they were still more firmly persuaded that the Arminians aimed at nothing less than the ruin of all religion; and hence they censured their magistrates with great warmth and freedom, for interposing their authority to promote peace and union with such adversaries. And those who are well informed and impartial must candidly acknowledge, that the Arminians were far from being sufficiently cautious in avoiding connections with persons of loose principles; and by frequenting the company of those whose sentiments were entirely different from the received doctrines of the Reformed church, they furnished their enemies with a pretext for suspecting their own principles, and representing their theological system in the worst colours."—(Mosheim, vol. v. p. 445.) It seems evident that they *patronized* men not only of loose principles, but of licentious character. The word *Calvinists* is not used in the historical preface of the Synod of Dort.

which weakness so increased upon him by degrees, that a short time after he departed this life. [Oct. 19, 1609.] Thus these contests and dissensions exercised the University and the churches of Batavia while Arminius was living; but when he was taken away from among the living, though every good man hoped that a great part of these evils would be taken away and buried along with him, seeing that he had been the leader and author of all these contentions; yet, as many pastors, every where in the churches of Holland, had consented to his opinion, and would not cease from propagating it, the deputies of the churches thought that nevertheless the convocation of a provincial Synod should be urged; to whom it was again answered, that the illustrious, the States, would then consider about calling some ecclesiastical convention, when the Classis of Alcmar had obeyed their mandates.

In the meantime, the pastors attached to Arminius, when they saw the affair brought into such a situation, that the calling of a Synod having been hindered, little seemed to be feared by them from ecclesiastical judgments and censures; as if with loosened reins of boldness and impudence, they began to inveigh and rage furiously, both in public and private, against the orthodox doctrine of the Reformed churches, concerning election, the perseverance of the saints, the assurance of salvation, and other articles, with the most bitter and contumelious revilings, with the greatest offence of the pious, and the congratulation of adversaries, and disturbance of the churches; and to render the doctrine of the churches by all means suspected by the people, and to embitter the minds, especially of the nobles (*magnatum*) against it, and the faithful teachers of the same. Neither was it sufficient for them by private whisperings, and public and official sermons (*tribunitiis*), to excite the minds, as well of the common people as of the rulers; but by public writings also, which in great number, and not with less scandal, were daily every where dispersed among the people, they so defamed (*proscindebant*, cut up) the doctrine of the Reformed churches, that the sworn adversaries of the same had scarcely been able to do it with greater virulence and evil speaking. And, that they might the better conciliate to themselves the favour of the magistrates, and render their minds more and more bitter against the rest of the pastors, by Utenbogardus at first, in a speech made in the convention of the illustrious, the States, and then publicly in writing, they endeavoured to persuade the magistrates that the rest of the pastors diminished and undermined the authority of the magistrates, and affected and arrogated to themselves a power collateral, or equal to their power.

Wherefore the deputies of the churches judged, that the illustrious, the States, should be again approached, and entreated that they would deign at length to apply a legal remedy to these evils, which seemed now to have come to the height, by calling together a Provincial Synod. And when the illustrious, the States, seemed easily about to consent, because of the extreme necessity of the matter, the pastors attached to the opinions of Arminius suggested to them a new counsel, by which they thought that this calling (of a Synod) might either be entirely hindered, or be so instituted that their cause might be in safety; namely, that the persons from among whom the Synod was to be called, should not be delegated by the churches, (as was equitable, and had been hitherto the custom,) but be called forth by the States themselves; for they would easily afterwards obtain that those only should be selected, who either were attached to their cause, or too little averse from it. This innovation, though they had already persuaded some of the chief persons of the country, the more prudent could not approve; who judged that this convocation (of a Synod) should be instituted after the accustomed manner. They effected, nevertheless, that while a disputation was excited among the illustrious, the States, concerning the manner of calling the Synod, that the convocation itself, (which in the first place these pastors regarded,) not only of the provincial Synod, but of the annual Synods, and those which before were ordinarily held, should by this means be entirely hindered. For as often as they who wished that these evils should be taken away from the churches by this lawful remedy, made mention concerning the convocation of any Synod; so often they who favoured Arminius and his cause renewed the contentions concerning the manner of calling it. Wherefore the pastors also, who were attached to the opinions of the same, (Arminius,) when they discerned that matters were now brought to that situation, that the fear of all ecclesiastical judgment and censure seemed to be taken away, being rendered more daring, their own churches not having been consulted, or aware of it, and without the authority of the supreme magistrate, they privately met together in a great number; and there, having entered into confederacy or conspiracy, by the subscription of names they formed a *body*, as they called it, separate from the body of the rest of their fellow pastors, and instituted a manifest schism in the Reformed churches. At this time they exhibited a suppliant writing, (*libellum,*) or, as they called it, the Remonstrance, to the illustrious, the States of Holland and West Friesland; from which they were afterwards called *Remonstrants.* In this they placed before them the doctrine of the Reformed churches, concerning the divine predestination, and the perseverance of the saints, unfaithfully, (*mala fide,*) and not without open and atrocious slanders,* that by this means they might render it odious to the illustrious orders; at the same time they added that declaration of their own opinion concerning the same articles, which they under the ambiguous coverings of words concealed, that so it might appear to the more unskilful not much distant from the truth. And moreover they petitioned from the illustrious, the States, to be received under their patronage and protection, against all the censures of the churches.

This matter vehemently affected all the Belgic churches with amazement and grief (*perculit*), as they saw that these controversies had now burst forth into an open schism; and they used every endeavour that they might be able to procure a copy of this *remonstrance*, by which means an answer might be returned to the calumnies of these persons. But by the favour of him who was used to keep these things, they (the Remonstrants) easily obtained, that not one copy could come into the hands of the rest of the pastors. Another thing was added to this calamity of the churches, which above measure increased their anxiety and their difficulties. For when a succes-

* It seems a sort of *right by prescription* to Anti-Calvinists, to misrepresent and bear false witness against the Calvinistic doctrines, and those who hold them. I would that no Calvinist had ever imitated them in this respect.

sor was sought to J. Arminius in the professorship of theology, the deputies of the churches strenuously requested and adjured the most ample the Directors of the University of Leyden, in the public name of the churches, that they would substitute in that place a man clear from all suspicion of heterodoxy, in order that by this means the controversies in the University of Leyden might gradually cease, and their peace be restored to the churches; at the same time they commended certain eminent theologians, as well foreign as Belgic, to the Directors, but without success (*irrito successu*). For the Remonstrants, who seem to have pre-occupied the minds of certain persons, effected by their commendations, that Conradus Vorstius, a professor of Steinfurt, a man for many years justly suspected by the Reformed churches of Socinianism, should be called to the professorship of theology in the place of Arminius; and for that cause that Utenbogardus should be sent away to Steinfurt. Which thing when the deputies of the churches had understood, they thought it to belong to their duty to admonish the illustrious, the States, that a man of this kind might not rashly be admitted to this vocation, who might be as a nail or claw in an ulcer, especially in so disturbed a state of the churches. Moreover, that this might be done by them with the greater fruit, they petitioned by letters from the venerable, the theological faculty of the University of Heidelberg, to whom this Vorstius had been intimately known, that it would sincerely declare, whether it thought that this Vorstius, in the present state of things, could with profit, and the peace and edification of the churches, be placed over the education of youth in the University of Leyden. It was also answered (by this theological faculty) that a certain book of his had lately been published concerning God and the divine attributes, in which he refuted (*convelleret*) the doctrine both of ancient and modern theologians; and taught that God was as to essence, great, finite, composed of essence and accident, changeable in his will, and obnoxious to passive power, (*passivæ potentiæ,*) with other similar portents. And that he had been sent ten years since to Heidelberg, that he might clear himself before the theological faculty, D. Pezelius also being present, from (*the charge*) of Socinianism, of which he had been accused by the churches. And indeed that he had so cleared himself, a writing (*syngrapha*) having been left: but that this clearing of himself (*purgationem*) had not been made valid, but, on the contrary, too often, and by various means, he had rendered himself more suspected, because he carried in his head a nest of monstrous fancies (*portentorum*), with which he had hitherto polluted the school and the youth at Steinfurt; but if a man of so suspected a faith should be called to the most illustrious University of Leyden, this would be nothing other than to extinguish a conflagration with oil.

When not only the deputies of the churches but also the most ample the magistrates of the principal cities of Holland, of Dort for instance, and Amsterdam, had signified these things to the lords the curators, and to the illustrious the States themselves, and entreated that they would not exasperate the difficulties of the churches, and expose them to the danger of new and greater (evils) by this calling of that man, the Remonstrants laboured with all their powers that they would not desist from this purposed calling (of him); for they persuaded them that this would be joined with the loss of their own authority. In the meantime, Vorstius came into Holland; who, after he had been heard in the convention of the illustrious, the States, Utenbogardus alone of the pastors being present, returned to Steinfurt.

About this time, when certain students of sacred theology, having been called to the ministry of the word in the divers Classes, were about to be subjected to examination, the Remonstrants procured it to be enjoined to these Classes, by the counsellors of the illustrious, the States, that no further declaration should be demanded from any one, in the examination, concerning the article of predestination, and the heads annexed to it, than what had been expressed in five articles of the Remonstrants, which were sent along with (this injunction); and at the same time, it was strictly forbidden, that any should be driven away from the ministry of those who professed that they thought in the before mentioned articles with the Remonstrants.* When the pastors, on many accounts,

* The five articles of the Remonstrants so often mentioned in this history, do not occur separately and all together in the authenticated documents, of which I make use; but comparing the detached accounts of them, and the arguments used in the Synod of Dort concerning them, with the following statement from Mosheim, (vol. v. pp. 444, 445,) the latter appears sufficiently accurate for our present purpose.

1. "That God, from all eternity, determined to bestow salvation on those who, as he foresaw, would persevere unto the end in their faith in Christ Jesus, and to inflict everlasting punishment on those who should continue in their unbelief, and resist, to the end of life, his divine succours.

2. "That Jesus Christ, by his death and sufferings, made an atonement for the sins of mankind in general, and of every individual in particular: that, however, none but those who believe in him can be partakers of that divine benefit.

were very reluctant, (*gravarentur,*) to consent to this, the deputies of the churches having been asked by them, laid open their grievances, in the next election of the illustrious, the States of Holland and West Friesland; and at the same time declared that they were prepared to prove in a lawful Synod that those articles of the Remonstrants were contrary to the word of God, and the Confession and Catechism of the Belgic churches; and they entreated the illustrious, the States, not to suffer these

---

3. "That *true faith* cannot proceed from the exercise of our natural faculties and powers, or from the force and operation of free will, since man, in consequence of his natural corruption, is incapable either of thinking or doing any good thing; and that therefore it is necessary to his conversion and salvation that he be *regenerated* and renewed by the operation of the Holy Ghost, which is the gift of God, through Jesus Christ.

4. "That this *divine grace,* or energy of the Holy Ghost, which heals the disorders of a corrupt nature, begins, advances, and brings to perfection every thing that can be called *good* in man; and that, consequently, all good works, without exception, are to be attributed to God alone, and to the operation of his grace: that, nevertheless, this grace does not *force* the man to act against his inclination, but may be *resisted* and rendered *ineffectual* by the perverse will of the impenitent sinner.

5. "That they who are united to Christ by faith, are thereby furnished with abundant strength, and with succours sufficient to enable them to triumph over the seductions of Satan, and the allurements of sin and temptation; but that the question, *Whether such may fall from their faith, and forfeit finally this state of grace,* has not been yet resolved with sufficient perspicuity, and must therefore be yet more carefully examined by an attentive study of what the holy Scriptures have declared in relation to this important point."

"It is to be observed, that this last article was afterwards changed by the Arminians, who, in process of time, declared their sentiments with less caution, and positively affirmed that *the saints might fall from a state of grace.*" Mosheim, vol. v. p. 445.

heterodox articles, having never been duly examined in a lawful assembly of the churches, to be obtruded in this manner on the churches; but rather, that they would call together the provincial Synod so often petitioned for, nay, now for a long time earnestly sought, in which these articles might be first examined according to the rule of the divine word. They showed also, with how great scandal and detriment of the churches it would be joined, if the appointed calling of Vorstius should proceed. And further they request, that this should be hindered by the authority of the illustrious, the States.

A consultation having been held concerning these things, it was determined that a conference should be appointed, at the next Comitia of the count of Hague, (*proximis Comitiis Hagæ-Comitis,*) in the convention itself of the illustrious, the States, on these five articles of the Remonstrants, between six pastors, to be chosen by each party. The Remonstrants had chosen for themselves, by the deputies of the several Classes, John Utenbogardus, of the Hague; Adrian Borrius, and John Arnoldi Corvin, of Leyden; Nicolas Grevinchovius, of Rotterdam; Edward Poppius, of Gouda, and Simon Episcopius, pastors of the church of Bleswick. But the rest of the pastors had chosen, by the deputies of each of the Classes, Peter Plancinus, of Amsterdam; Libertus Francinus, of Brilan; Ruardus Acronius, of Schiedam; John Beccius, of Dort; John Bogardus, of Harlem; and Festus Hommius, of Leyden, pastors of the church.

March 11, 1611.] When they had met together, the Remonstrants refused to institute the conference with the other six pastors, as with the deputies of the Classes of Holland and West Friesland, such as they showed themselves to be by letters of commission (*fidei*), lest they should seem to be the adversaries of the churches: moreover they protested that they would depart, the matter being left unfinished, (*re infecta,*) unless these would lay aside that character. When there had been for a long time much disputation, the rest of the pastors chose rather to yield to their importunity, than to contend any longer concerning that matter. And they who had been deputed by the Classes, before they went into the conference, besought the illustrious lords, the States, that the promise which had been made to the churches more than two years before, in the conference held between Arminius and Gomarus, (namely, that the conference being ended the judgment of this cause might be permitted and reserved to a provincial, or national Synod,) might here also be renewed.

It was agreed upon that this order of proceeding should be observed by them; that each party should comprise in writing the arguments of its own opinion, concerning which a conference should then be instituted by word of mouth. Before they came to the examination of the articles, the pastors, who we before said had been deputed by the Classes, exhibited an answer to the suppliant writing (*libellum*) of the Remonstrants, a copy of which they had procured a little before the conference; in which they showed, that the Remonstrants had most unfaithfully (*pessimâ fide*) set forth the opinion of the Reformed churches, and had feigned in addition to it (*adfinxisse*) many things as a calumny; and that they had not openly avowed their own (opinion), or set forth all the articles concerning which there was a controversy. And, seeing there were more controverted heads, besides those which were explained in these five articles, they humbly prayed, that, by the authority of the illustrious, the States, it might be enjoined on the Remonstrants, that they should likewise roundly and openly declare themselves concerning all the rest. Therefore, when the first article of the Remonstrants was about to be discussed, (or canvassed, *excutiendus*) in which it is stated, "that God had from eternity decreed to save persevering believers," which no Christian denies, and this article was so placed by them, as that which contained the doctrine concerning God's eternal election, the Remonstrants were asked, that (in addition) to the declaration of their opinion, as expressed in this article, they would explain these two things: First, whether they would maintain that this article contained the whole decree of predestination; secondly, whether they thought that this faith and perseverance in the faith were *causes* and *conditions* which *preceded* election unto salvation; or *fruits* which *spring from* election, and follow after it. After they had shifted about for some time, they answered at length, to the first indeed, that they acknowledged no other predestination to salvation, than that which had been expressed by them in the first article; but to the second, that faith in the consideration and view of God was prior to election to salvation, and that it did not follow in the manner of any fruit. They then proposed in return seven other questions, as well concerning election as reprobation, to which they desired an answer to be given by the pastors deputed from the Classes. These, as they did not belong to the state of the controversy concerning the first article, and moreover were most of them mutilated and intricate, were proposed by them, that by this method they might draw them from the principal state of the controversy, and the right manner of treating it into doubtful disputations (*ambages*).* The pastors, having shown by a libel (*libellum*) to the illustrious, the States, this unjust way of proceeding, did not indeed entreat that they might not manifest their own opinion concerning reprobation; as the Remonstrants had too often iniquitously (*improbè*) objected to the same persons; but declared expressly their opinion, as far as they thought might suffice for the peace and edification of the churches, not only by word of mouth, but also in writing; that indeed when they state the eternal decree concerning the election of individual persons, they at the same time state the eternal decree concerning the reprobation or rejection of certain individual persons; because it could not be, that there should be election, but moreover there must be, at the same time, a certain reprobation or dereliction. Yet to rashly canvass all these difficult questions concerning this article, was nothing else but to fill the church with useless disputations and contentions not profitable, and to disturb its peace. That this their declaration suppliantly expressed in this libel, ought to suffice all men of moderate dispositions and lovers of peace: namely, that it was indeed believed and taught by them, that God condemned no one; yea, neither had he decreed to condemn any one, unless justly for his own proper sins.†

---

* A common method among many controversialists, expressly called "throwing dust in men's eyes."

† "That God, by an absolute decree, had elected to salvation a very small number of men, without any regard to their faith and obedience whatever; and secluded from saving grace all the rest of mankind, and appointed them by the same decree to eternal damnation, without any regard to their infidelity or impenitency." Heylin's 1st Article of the Synod of Dort.

It therefore pleased the illustrious, the States, that leaving these thorny questions, they should come to the discussion of the articles. The pastors deputed by the churches proposed in writing their reasons on account of which they disapproved of each of these articles. The Remonstrants also, on the other side, exhibited in writing their own arguments, by which they thought that each of them might be confirmed. About these reasons and arguments, disputations were held by speaking in the full convention of the illustrious, the States. The parts of the collocutor, in the name of those deputed by the churches, were sustained by Festus Hommius; but in the name of the Remonstrants, at first by Adrian Borrius, and then by Nicolas Grevinchovius, John Arnoldi, and Simon Episcopius, succeeding each other by turns.

While the pastors were occupied in this conference, Conradus Vorstius had returned out of Westphalia into Holland, whom the illustrious, the States, appointed to be heard in a full convention, all the collocutors being present. When they were come together, he made a prolix oration, in which he endeavoured to clear himself from the errors objected to him. Then the collocutors were asked whether they had any considerations on account of which they judged that the calling of Vorstius to the professorship of theology in the University of Leyden should be hindered. The Remonstrants expressly declared that they had nothing against Vorstius, neither had they detected any thing in his writings which was repugnant to truth and piety.* The other pastors exhibited in writing

* "Among the persecuted ecclesiastics was the famous Vorstius, who by his religious sentiments, which differed but little from the Socinian system, had rendered the Arminians particularly odious." Mosheim, vol. v. p. 455.

their reasons for which they judged that this vocation would be vehemently mischievous and disgraceful to the churches of Holland; and they showed from a book of Socinus, concerning the authority of the sacred Scriptures, edited by Vorstius himself, and interpolated, and also from that which Vorstius himself had very lately written and published concerning God and the divine attributes, his principal errors, concerning which there was held during some days a conference between him and Festus Hommius, in the convention of the illustrious, the States, in the presence of the collocutors. This having been finished, the pastors on each side were again asked by the illustrious, the States, that they would sincerely, and without any passions (*affectibus*), declare whether Vorstius by his answers seemed to have satisfied them. The Remonstrants answered, that full satisfaction had been given to them by Vorstius, and they moreover judged that it would be very useful to the churches and to the University if his vocation proceeded. The rest of the pastors declared in writing, that the answers of Vorstius were so far from having moved them from their former opinion, that by them they were the more confirmed in that opinion, and that his vocation could not be forwarded, except by the extreme detriment of the churches and of the University, and the manifest danger of still greater disturbance, to which, that they might not rashly expose the churches by this vocation, they submissively adjured (or *obtested*) the illustrious, the States, that, dismissing Vorstius, they might return to the conference concerning the five articles of the Remonstrants: and when this, having been continued during some days, was at length brought to a conclusion, the illustrious, the States, commanded the collocutors on each side, that those things which had been spoken *viva voce*, and whatever they might judge necessary to a more full answer, being on each side comprised in writing, should by Utenbogardus and Festus be exhibited to the illustrious, the States. And in the meantime, that the pastors might not glory among themselves concerning the victory which they had gained one over the other, but that they might teach moderately with edification concerning the controverted articles, and live among themselves in peace and charity, they determined that these articles should be left in the same state in which they had been before the conference.

In the cause of Vorstius nothing was at that time decided, but when a little time afterwards the most ample, the magistrates, of the city of Dort, by their delegates, most ample men, D. Hugo Musius, ab Holii, the Prætor, (or Mayor,) James Wittius, Adrian Repelarius, John Berkius, the Syndic, requested the illustrious, the States, seeing rumours concerning the errors and heresies of Vorstius, became daily more and more frequent, that his vocation might be broken off, or at least deferred; the illustrious, the States, commanded the curators of the University to proceed no further in his vocation. And when the report of his vocation had come to James the First himself, the most serene and powerful king of Great Britain, the Defender of the Faith, who out of his admirable skill in theological matters, especially in a king, and for his singular zeal towards the Reformed religion, when he had himself carefully read the tract of Vorstius, concerning God, and had noted the principal errors with his own hand, judged that the illustrious, the High Mightinesses the States General, his neighbours and his allies, were to be admonished, as well by letters (the catalogue of his errors being also transmitted,) as by his own ambassador, an illustrious person, D. Rodolphus Winwood, not to admit a man infamous by so many and so great errors and blasphemies, to the public office of teaching in the University; but rather to banish him from their borders, lest if the youth should be imbued by him with these wicked and execrable errors, the state should by little and little go to decay; seeing that by the purity of the Reformed doctrine, in which the Belgic churches had hitherto cultivated an amicable agreement with the English, and in the preservation of it, the safety of the republic itself was concerned.* When this was delayed, the Remonstrants earnestly striving against it, and especially Vorstius, by various explanations, apologies, prologues (*prodromis*,) and answers, as well modest, as more fully excusing and strengthening (*incrustante*) his own errors; yet his most Serene Royal Majesty did not desist to urge his dismission, sometimes repeating his admonitions, and even adding a serious protestation.†

---

* This at least shows the general judgment of theologians concerning Vorstius, whom the Remonstrants so zealously supported; and even still more strongly, on the supposition that James and his select divines were not at that time favourable to Calvinism.

† This shows that the generally received *doctrine* of the church of England was then supposed to be, viz. for substance the same as that of the Belgic church. The eulogium on James I. reminds us of the words of Cowper, "Grant me discernment, I allow it you:" yet the English divines have spoken still more decidedly on the subject. (Preface to Translation of the Bible.) It may be supposed, that the Belgic divines who adhered to the Synod of Dort, would retract or qualify this eulogium, when they learned the change which soon after took place in England under the patronage of the same James.

While these things were doing, certain students of sacred theology, who likewise had come forth from the instruction and the house of Vorstius, in the University of Franeker, which they had now been sedulously employed in infecting with Socinian errors, published in print a certain little book of Faustus Socinus, concerning the duty of a Christian man, in which persuasions are given, that all who would consult the salvation of their own souls, having deserted the dogmas and assemblies of the Reformed churches, should embrace the opinion of the Photinians and the Ebionites, adding a preface, in which they diligently commend this book unto the churches.* The illustrious, the States of Friesland, having been assured of this, and having at the same time procured certain familiar letters of these students, in which they declared by what arts the common cause of Socinianism, (which they not obscurely intimated was also carried on by Vorstius and by Utenbogardus and others in Holland,) might be occultly and safely propagated; having taken care that the most of these copies of this book should be destroyed by the avenging flames, and having expelled the students from their confines, they, at first indeed by letters, admonished the magistrates of the principal cities of Holland, and then by the most noble person Kempson a Donia, the illustrious lords, the States, themselves; and they requested, inasmuch as the orthodox

* "Photinus's opinions concerning the Deity were equally repugnant to the orthodox and Arian systems."—(See Mosheim, vol. i. pp. 425, 426.) Though the Ebionites believed the celestial mission of Christ, and his participation of a divine nature, yet they regarded him as a man born of Joseph and Mary, according to the ordinary course of nature."—(Ibid. vol. i. pp. 214, 215.)

consent in the Reformed doctrine was the principal bond and foundation of union among the confederated provinces, that they would not admit, by the vocation of one man, thus suspected of manifest heresies, this agreement to be enfeebled, nor suffer themselves to be led about by artifices and frauds of this kind, by which it was evident that these men secretly attempted this. But the pastors of Leoward having made public the above mentioned letters of the students, with necessary annotations, solemnly warned all the churches to take heed to themselves against artifices of this kind, and especially the deceitful machinations of the heretics, and in the first place of Vorstius. The illustrious duchy of Guelderland and county of Zutphen also warned the illustrious, the States of Holland, concerning the same thing, who answered that nothing would be more their hearty desire and care, than that they might retain in the common business of religion this consent, with the rest of the federated provinces, inviolate. Concerning which their constant purpose, they peculiarly requested that their federated neighbours would be assured; in the meantime, that they themselves would have regard to this admonition. And they command Vorstius to remove his place of abode from the city of Leyden to Gouda, and there to vindicate himself from the errors objected to him by public writings, as much as he could.

Then the same, the lords the States, decreed, that they who held the conference at the Hague should on each side exhibit in writing the state of the controversy concerning the five articles of the Remonstrants; and should at the same time add their counsels, by what method they thought that these controversies might be most advantageously composed to the peace of the church and the good of the republic. The Remonstrants judged, that no more certain method of concord could be entered on than a mutual toleration, by which each party might be permitted freely to teach and contend for his own opinion concerning these articles.* The other pastors declared that they could not show a more advantageous way, than that as soon as possible, and on the first opportunity, a national Synod should be called together by the authority of the illustrious, the High Mightinesses, the States General; in which these and all other controversies having been clearly explained and examined, it might be determined which opinion agreed with the word of God, and the common judgment of the Reformed churches, and on that account ought to be publicly taught, lest by the agitating of discordant opinions, truth should be injured, or the peace of the churches disturbed.

On these counsels the opinions of the illustrious, the States, were various, some approving the counsel of the Remonstrants, and others that of the rest of the pastors, which was the cause that nothing was determined in this

* Such a toleration amounted to an entire abolition of the Belgic Confession and Catechism, without any previous interference of those Synods, Classes, and Presbyteries, which were essential to their form of church-government. As if, under the name of toleration, here in England, the whole establishment of the church, without any reference to the authority which established it, should be disannulled by one royal or senatorial mandate, and all preferments in the church and universities thrown open to men of every creed and character. James the Second attempted a little in this way in order to bring in popery, but the dissenters in general opposed this his dispensing power, and few, if any, of modern dissenters, who make the highest claims of something above toleration, mean such a complete abolition of the present state of things, by the same despotic authority as this implied.

matter, by which an end might be put to these controversies.

Dec. 3, 1611.] But when the illustrious, the States, had understood that, besides these five articles, concerning many other things controversies of no small importance were moved, in order that they might meet the innovations maturely, they appointed that the doctrine of the holy Gospel of our Lord Jesus Christ should be most purely set forth, as well in the churches as in the public schools of these regions; and to this end, in the churches and in the public schools of Holland and West Friesland; that concerning the perfect satisfaction of our Saviour Jesus Christ for our sins, concerning the justification of man before God, concerning saving faith and original sin, and the certitude of salvation, and the perfection of man in this life, nothing should be taught otherwise than as it is every where delivered in the Reformed churches, and hath been hitherto delivered in these provinces. In the meanwhile, every where in the churches, discords, scandals, disturbances and confusions increased in a deplorable manner. For the Remonstrants laboured assiduously with all their powers, that the pastors who especially resisted their attempts, (the magistrates having been excited against them by false accusations,) should not only be cast out of their ministerial stations, but out of the cities themselves; and that on all the churches which were deprived of pastors, even when reluctant and struggling against it, those should be obtruded who were addicted to their own opinions, all others being excluded wherever they were able, though excellently furnished with learning, piety, and necessary endowments, and lawfully sought out and called by the church.* And this was the cause that the orthodox churches could not consider, as their lawful pastors, pastors of this kind; who had either oppressed and cast out their innocent colleagues, contrary to all law and justice, or who had been obtruded on them against their will, and who had reviled the doctrine of the Reformed churches, in the most virulent sermons, daily and in a horrid manner; that they could not hear their sermons, or partake of the Lord's supper, along with the same; but that they chose rather to go to the sermons of orthodox pastors in the adjacent places, though they were exposed to many reproaches, disgraces, and injuries on that account. And these were the beginnings and occasions of the separations from the Remonstrants.†

The church at Alcmar was the first among all, which was compelled to institute a separation of this kind. For Adolphus Venator, the pastor of that church, having been suspended from the office of teaching, as well for his too impure life, as for his most impure doctrine, by the churches of North Holland, despising the censures of the churches, nevertheless persisted in the office of teaching. And now that the magistracy having been changed, as it was used to be done every year, such persons had been lawfully chosen as seemed least to favour his party, and

* The toleration which these men pleaded for, was precisely like that which Papists demand as emancipation—that is, power and full liberty to draw over others to their party by every artful means, till they become strong enough to refuse toleration to all other men.

† Here was a schism begun, as several others have been; but did all the blame lie on those who separated from the rest? On the other hand, would such a toleration as is here described meet the wishes and claims of the advocates for toleration, who in this transaction, as in many others, are imposed upon by a favourite term, however misapplied?

on whose patronage he could no longer depend; having excited the people against the lawful magistracy, he effected that they (the common people), having seized arms by sedition, would not be appeased, before the lawful magistracy, having abdicated themselves, certain others were substituted to the same, men estranged from the Reformed religion, and addicted to the party of Venator. These men, as soon as they had been established in the government of the city, at Venator's instigation, at first commanded the elders and deacons to go out of their office; and then they also deprived of their ministerial stations two pastors, because they had opposed themselves against the errors of Venator; of whom the one, Peter Cornelii, for almost fifty years had presided over that church with the greatest edification; the other, Cornelius Hillenius, a man of the most upright faith and life, and a very earnest (*acerrimum*) defender of the orthodox doctrine, they most unworthily cast forth as driven out of the city. This separation (at Alcmar) the church at Rotterdam was compelled to imitate; for Nicolas Grevinchovius, when he saw his colleague, Cornelius Gezelius, most acceptable to the church at Rotterdam, on account of his singular piety, modesty, and sincerity, and that by his endeavours he vehemently resisted the introduction of the doctrine of the Remonstrants, procured, that by the magistracy of that place, he should first be deprived of his ministry, and then driven out of the city by the public beadles (*lictores*).* The pastors also of the Classis of Rotterdam, at-

* The names both of the persecuted and persecuting pastors are given in this history; but the names of the magistrates who concurred in the persecution are withheld, in honour, as it may seem, of the magistracy. This greatly accords to the narrative in the Acts of the Apostles.

tached to the purity of doctrine, declined holding the meetings of the Classis with this Grevinchovius, and others who had been drawn over by him to the opinion of the Remonstrants, when the magistracy of Rotterdam by authority had obtruded Simon Episcopius, to whom the church of Amsterdam, in which he had lived, had refused to give a testimonial of doctrine and life, on the unwilling church of Bleyswick, contrary to the preferable (*potiora*) suffrages of the pastors. Many churches also in the villages, on which either Remonstrants had been obtruded against their will, or whose pastors had revolted to the Remonstrants, because they could not hear without the greatest offence, and sorrow, and perturbation of mind, those horrid railings against the orthodox doctrine, which were daily heard in their sermons, having left their temples they either went to the sermons of the neighbouring orthodox pastors, or where these could not be had at their own villages, they were instructed by other pastors, or by orthodox candidates for the ministry, in separated assemblies; which when the Remonstrants had in vain attempted to hinder by the edicts of their magistrates, they excited no small persecution against these churches.*

In the mean time, the lords, the curators of the University of Leyden, by the counsel of the Remonstrants, called M. Simon Episcopius to the professorship of theology, that very renowned man, Dr. John Polyander, who had been called to the same professorship in the place of

* This was their *toleration!* Certainly, according to this history, the persecution *began* on the part of the Remonstrants; nor does the contrary appear, that I can learn, from other histories. The Contra-Remonstrants appealed to existing laws and to legal Synods; the Remonstrants used the illegal aid of penal edicts and secular magistrates.

F. Gomarus, being unwilling, and struggling against it. This augmented not a little the grief and anxiety of the churches; when from this it appeared that it was determined by them, (the curators,) to cherish contentions in that University, and to establish the doctrine of the Remonstrants. But as these evils now could scarcely any longer be contained within the limits of the churches of Holland, this contagion at length pervaded, in the first place, the neighbouring churches of Gueldria, the province of Utrecht and Transylvania. In the diocese of Utrecht, by the negligence of the pastors, the ecclesiastical order seemed prostrated. And under the pretext of restoring it, Utenbogardus introduced into that church some Remonstrant pastors, and among them one James Taurinus, a fierce and turbulent man. These (pastors) from that time gave diligence, not only in this city, but in the whole province, by ejecting everywhere the orthodox pastors, and substituting Remonstrants in their places, that the doctrine of the Remonstrants alone should publicly prevail. But in order to establish their cause in the same province, they devised a new formula of ecclesiastical government, which at first had been approved by the Synod, in which Utenbogardus, the pastor of the Hague, presided, and then, through the endeavour of the same person, by the illustrious, the States, of that province likewise. In the fourth and fifth article of the second chapter, the toleration of the opinion of the Remonstrants, which in Holland they so greatly urged, was established; where also the doctrine of the Reformed churches is obliquely and odiously traduced. Finally, very many new things in the government of the churches occur everywhere in this formula. So that from the same it might appear, that nothing other was proposed by these men, than that they might make all things new, not only in doctrine, but in the external government of the church by rites (*gubernatione ritibus ecclessiæ.*)

And now also in Gueldria, the Remonstrants had drawn over to their party, the pastors of Neomagen, Bommelien, and Tilan; who from that time placed over the ministerial charges of the neighbouring churches, only men of their own opinion, and that they might do this with the more freedom and safety, Utenbogardus, Borrius, and Taurinus, going into Gueldria, when the comitia of the illustrious, the States, were celebrated in the same place, with the other Remonstrants effected this, that in the province also, the ordinary and annual meeting of the Synods should be prevented. In Transylvania also, some pastors, especially in the church of Campen and Daventer, by the endeavours and artifices of certain persons, had been drawn over to the opinion of the Remonstrants, who in those places thenceforth disturbed peaceable churches with new contentions.

Sept. 27, 1612.] When the Belgic churches saw that this evil, thus crept also into the other provinces, was spread abroad in them, as they judged it to be most highly necessary that it should be met as soon as possible, neither that the remedy should be any longer deferred, having communicated counsels one with another, they sent away two delegates from each of the provinces, to the illustrious, the High Mightinesses, the States General: namely, from Gueldria, John Fontanus and William Baudartius; from Holland, Libertus Fraxinus and Festus Hommius; from Zealand, Herman Frankelius and William Telingius; those of Utrecht refused to send theirs; from Friesland,

Gellius Acronius and Godofrid Sopingius; from Transylvania, John Gosmannus and John Langius; finally, from the state of Groningen and Omland, Cornelius Hillenius and Wolfgang Agricola, who, together with the deputies of the church of Amsterdam, which was Synodal, Peter Plancius, and John Hallius, having set forth copiously the difficulties and dangers of the churches, as well in the name of the churches themselves as also most of them in the name of the illustrious, the States, of their own provinces, (whose letters also they set before them,) most strenuously requested and adjured the illustrious, their High Mightinesses, the States General, that pitying the most afflicted state of the churches, they would at length seriously think concerning a remedy of these evils; and for that purpose at the earliest time call together a national Synod, (which had been) first promised many years before. Though most persons among the States General judged, that the convocation (of a Synod) was not to be deferred any longer, and even themselves urged it: yet because the delegates of the province of Utrecht were absent, and those of Holland and West Friesland said that they had not been furnished with mandates sufficently clear as to that business, by those who delegated them, the matter was put off, until the delegates of all the provinces had agreed to it by their common suffrages, which was thenceforth hindered from being done by the endeavour of the Remonstrants in Holland and Utrecht.

In the meantime, the Remonstrants did not desist from strenuously promoting their own cause, (or cease) to court (*aucupari*) the favour of the great men, to occupy the minds of the magistrates, to render suspected to the politicians and impede all Synodical meetings, to seize on the vacant churches, to propagate their own opinion by sermons and public writings, to rail at the orthodox doctrine with horrid calumnies, to draw over the people to their party, and to alienate them more and more from the doctrine of the Reformed churches. For this purpose they earnestly scattered pamphlets (*libellos*) in great number, among the common people, written in the vulgar tongue, under the titles of "The bells of a conflagration," (*campanæ incendiariæ*) "A more compressed declaration," "A more direct way," and others; in which they not only fought in defence of their own doctrine, but both excused Vorstius, and most atrociously, with a canine eloquence, canvassed the received doctrine of the Belgic churches by most impudent calumnies, and most absurd consequences deduced wickedly and unjustly against the same. Hence bitter disputes and altercations were excited among the people, which sounded throughout all places; and the minds also of those who were most nearly related, (or connected, *conjunctissimorum*) having been embittered among themselves, (with the great wound of charity, and the disturbance of the churches and of the public peace, and with the immense grief and offence of the pious,) were torn asunder in the most miserable manner. And as in most of the cities, they had the magistracy more favourable to them, and could do every thing, through J. Utenbogardus, with the advocate of Holland, they insolently exulted over the churches, and their fellow ministers.

In the meanwhile, all pious men, and lovers of their country and of religion, bewailed and wept over this most wretched calamity of the churches; and when they could not in their mind perceive whither at length these tumults were about to grow, unless a remedy should be maturely applied, because this had not hitherto been practicable by public authority, they began seriously to think, whether by some other way this evil might at least be stopped, if it could not be taken away. In the first place, the most illustrious, the count of Nassau, William Lewis, the Governor of Friesland, according to his extraordinary affection toward the churches and the republic, privately admonished as well Utenbogardus on the one side, as Festus Hommius on the other, that, seeing the state of the republic itself grievously assaulted by these ecclesiastical contentions, they should look well to it, in a friendly and brotherly manner between themselves, to see whether some honourable way might not be found out, of composing this most deplorable dissension, and of coming to an agreement. Festus declared, that if the Remonstrants differed from the rest of the pastors in no other articles than in those five concerning predestination, and the heads annexed to it, he thought that a way might be found out in which some peace might be established between the parties, until the whole controversy should be settled by a national Synod. But because there were weighty reasons on account of which the churches believed that most of the Remonstrants dissented from the doctrine of the Belgic churches in more articles, and those of greater importance, neither could it be done (*fieri*) that under the pretext of these five articles they should permit or suffer the most grievous errors to be brought into the same (churches), there did not seem any hope of entering into agreement with the Remonstrants, unless they would sincerely (or unreservedly, *sincerè*) declare, that except these five articles, they thought with the Reformed Belgic churches in all the heads of doctrine.* Utenbogardus being interrogated as to these things, answered, that as far as he himself was concerned, he had nothing, beyond these five articles, in which he dissented, and that he would be always ready to declare sincerely his own opinion, nor did he doubt but that the most of the Remonstrants would do the same, and that he did not wish for any thing more, than that for this cause a conference might be instituted among some pastors of a more moderate disposition. And when he had repeated the same declaration privately to Festus at Leyda, it was agreed between them, that each of them should procure among his own friends, three pastors to be deputed on each side, who might in a friendly manner confer together, and seriously consider among themselves concerning a convenient way of peace, which afterwards might be communicated to the churches, and approved by them.

Feb. 27, A. D. 1613.] When the illustrious, the States of Holland, understood that these counsels were privately agitated, they approved this their earnest endeavour, and commanded in the public name, that this conference should be held as soon as it could be done. Soon after, there met together, for this cause, in the city

* As predestination, and the doctrines immediately and evidently connected with it, are more readily rendered odious in the view of mankind in general, than the other peculiar doctrines of Christianity, at that time, as well as at present, it was the policy of those whose real and declared views were opposed to others of these doctrines, to hold out to the public, and to rulers especially, that the whole dispute, or difference, was about election and reprobation, while in refuting these articles they take in a much wider compass. But an obnoxious word will do a great deal of execution on those who have not time or heart to examine the matter deeply.

of Delft, on the part of the Remonstrants, John Utenbogardus, Adrian Borrius, and Nicolas Gervinchovius; on the part of the rest of the pastors, John Beccius, John Bogardus, and Festus Hommius. After that the illustrious, the States had, by their delegates, exhorted them seriously, that laying aside all resentments and evil affections, they would bend the whole energy of their capacity, that some way of peace among themselves might be found; and had declared that this would be at the same time acceptable to God, and to the churches and all pious men, and in the first place to themselves, the illustrious, the States; and when each of these pastors had testified that they came together with a mind most earnestly desirous of peace, and that they would bring thither all things which could proceed from them, in order to conciliate peace, an amicable conference was held by them. In this the Remonstrants declared, that they were not able to show any other way of peace, except a mutual toleration, as they called it: namely, that it should be freely permitted to each party, to teach publicly his own opinion concerning those five articles; and they asked of the rest of the pastors, to declare whether they thought their opinion, expressed in these five articles, to be tolerable or not. If they thought that it was not tolerable, (or to be tolerated,) it was not necessary that any further deliberation should be had concerning the way of peace; as truly in their judgment, no method then would remain of entering into peace. The rest of the pastors answered, that this appeared to them the safest and most advantageous way of peace; that seeing they were each of them pastors of the Reformed Belgic churches, and were desirous of being considered as such, each party should submit its own cause to the lawful decision of the Belgic churches, and that it should for that end and purpose, seriously and sincerely labour that a national Synod of the Reformed churches should be called together as speedily as might be, even if it could be done in the next summer, by the authority of the illustrious and High Mightinesses, the States General, in which the whole cause having been lawfully examined and discussed, it might either be determined which doctrine, as agreeable to the word of God, ought thenceforth to be taught in the churches, or that the plan of a toleration might be entered into, by the suffrages of all the churches of that kind which might appear proper to be instituted from the word of God. That they were ready to subject themselves to the judgment of the Synod, if the Remonstrants were willing to do the same, thus peace might be accomplished; but that a toleration such as they had hitherto used, and such as they seemed to request, being circumscribed by no laws, could not promote the peace of the churches, but if they would suffer it to be circumscribed with fair (or *honourable*) conditions, they were ready to confer with them concerning the same (conditions), provided they would assure the churches by a sincere and open declaration, that they thought differently from these Reformed churches in no other heads of doctrine except these five articles.* But since the illustrious,

* "The demands of the Arminians were moderate; they required no more than a bare toleration of their religious sentiments; and some of the first men in the republic, such as Olden Barneveldt, Grotius, Hoogerberts, and several others, looked upon this demand as just and reasonable." (Mosheim, vol. v. p. 442.) "This toleration was offered to them in the conference holden at the Hague in 1611, provided they would renounce the errors of Socinianism." Note by Maclaine.

the States, two years before, [Dec. 3, 1611,] had by name expressed six heads of doctrine, concerning which they forbad to be taught, otherwise than it had been hitherto delivered to the Belgic churches, namely, concerning the perfect satisfaction of our Lord Jesus Christ for our sins, the justification of man before God, saving faith, original sin, the assurance (or certitude) of salvation, and concerning the perfection of man in this life, they, in the first place, demanded that they would declare concerning these articles, that they embraced the opinion expressed in the Confession and Catechism of these churches, which they, the other pastors, had comprised from the same in certain written theses, and that they rejected the contrary opinion proposed in certain anti-theses, from the writings of Arminius, Bertius, Vorstius, Venator, and others. The Remonstrants replied (*regesserunt*) to this, that they could not see in what manner these controversies could be quieted (*sopiri*) by a national Synod; and truly in the present state of things, that they neither approved nor demanded its convocation; that this cause could not be helped by synodal decisions; nor did they think that Holland, in the concern of religion, would ever submit itself to the decisions of the other provinces. As to the declaration which was demanded, they would communicate with the other Remonstrants concerning the same, and when on each side they had comprised briefly in writing their own opinion, they departed, the business being left unfinished.* Afterwards the illustrious, the States, called

* The event was what might previously have been expected: indeed nothing else could come of such a conference, between parties whose sentiments were so entirely discordant (2 Cor. vi. 16—18.) The toleration demanded by the Remonstrants was in direct opposition to the

Utenbogardus and Festus to them, that they might know from them what had been done in this conference at Delft, and what hopes shone forth of concord being entered on. Festus sincerely and without disguise (*nudèque*) related what had been done, and declared that hope of peace shone forth, only provided the Remonstrants would openly declare their opinion on the articles delivered to them. Utenbogardus, by courtly craftiness, had procured that he should be heard alone, Festus being absent, that he might the more freely propose the things which he thought would serve his own purpose. And when he had odiously traduced the proceedings of the rest of the pastors, as the persons who, by the demand of a declaration, (which yet before the conference he himself had promised,) endeavoured to bring a new inquisition into the churches, and one by no means to be endured, obtained that the same persons should be forbidden any more to demand this declaration from the Remonstrants, and moreover, that it should at the same time be enjoined on them to explain more at large in writing their counsel on the best way of peace, and concerning the conditions by which they thought that a toleration should be circumscribed. When this had been done by them, and it had also been shown that the proposed *theses* concerning which a declaration had been demanded, were extant in so many words in the Confession and Catechism of the Belgic

---

existing laws, grounded on private or partial authority at best, like King James's claim of the dispensing power over acts of parliament in matters of religion, and indeed it amounted to a private repeal of those laws. The others were willing to consent to a legal and limited toleration. It is also evident that their firm decision and opposition was not mainly about predestination and reprobation.

churches; and the *anti-theses* themselves had been delivered in public writings by many persons with whom the Remonstrants had much communication in these regions;* when this their writing had been publicly read, they (the Remonstrants) by their advocate effected that it should be severely forbidden to be communicated to any of the human race, either in printing, or as written by the hand of any one. And because they saw that the deputies of the churches, or of the Synods, to whom the common cause of these concerns used to be committed, greatly withstood them, (as the nature of their office demanded,) they caused also, that as before all the annual Synods had been hindered, so that it should likewise be forbidden to the same persons, henceforth to use the name, or perform the office, of a *deputy* of the churches or of a Synod. That by this means all care respecting the safety and peace of the churches being taken away, they (the Remonstrants) might so much the more freely make progress among them.†

* Mosheim and many (indeed *most*) other writers on the subject, represent the Contra-Remonstrants as aiming to impose the creed of Geneva, or of Calvin, on the Remonstrants in Belgium. Let the impartial reader judge whether this was the real case. There might be, and indeed was, some coincidence between this and the Confession and Catechism of the Belgic churches, but the latter exclusively are mentioned in the whole contest.

† These decrees were made by the States of Holland alone or nearly, and they directly tended to disannul the code of laws of the federated provinces, promulged by the States General of these provinces, and thus to dissolve their political as well as religious union. Now what motives could the Remonstrants or their patrons have, in such circumstances, for so carefully concealing the statements and avowed sentiments of the other pastors? Impartial love of the truth could not possibly suggest such precautions and injunctions. They cannot

By this method of acting, the Remonstrants rendered themselves more and more suspected by the churches; while all the more prudent men judged that unless they dissented in these articles (the six stated above, pp. 125, 137,) from the doctrine of the churches, they would have had no reason why they should covertly flee from this declaration; especially when they might have (thus) promoted (*consuli posset*) the peace of the churches and their own credit. But that they might the more easily obtain that toleration by public authority which they always pressed; by the benefit of which they indeed hoped to be able by little and little to introduce their own doctrine in the churches, they employed this artifice; they sent over into England, by Hugo Grotius, a certain writing, in which the true state of the controversy was dissembled, a copy of a letter being also annexed; and they requested that he would petition from the most Serene James, King of Great Britain, seeing this cause could not be settled by any other method than by a toleration, that his most Serene royal Majesty would deign to give letters according to the form of the annexed copy, to the illustrious, the High Mightinesses the States General; which he, (Grotius) having seized on an opportunity, surreptitiously obtained, and transmitted them to the illustrious, the States General.*

---

but call to our recollection the conduct of the Jewish priests and rulers respecting the apostles of Christ, "But that it spread no further among the people, let us straitly threaten them, that they speak to no man in this name." (Acts iv. 16, 17.)

* It should be noted that this narrative was published several years before the death of James, who, therefore, it must be presumed, was willing to have it thought that these letters were surreptitiously obtained by Grotius; and indeed he seems to have been enveigled

On this occasion, the Remonstrants exulted after a wonderful manner, and hoping that they might now become possessed of their wish, they laboured by their advocate, that a certain formula of a toleration (the same indeed which is contained in the fourth and fifth articles of the second chapter of the ecclesiastical government of Utrecht,) should be confirmed by the authority of the illustrious, the States, and commanded to the churches. Though the minds of many in the convention of the States were inclined to this, yet the more prudent strenuously opposed it; thinking it to be unjust to command (authoritatively) on the church a toleration, as to articles of faith which had never been duly examined in a lawful ecclesiastical convention, and which drew with them a manifest change in doctrine; neither could the peace of the churches be obtained by this, when it was to be feared, if it were permitted, that opinions so discordant should be proposed from the same pulpit to the same congregations, that the churches should be more and more disturbed, as experience had hitherto taught.* Yet the Re-

into a measure, by no means consistent with the part which he afterwards sustained in the controversy.

* Let it be recollected that all the parties were *professedly*, and many of them *in judgment and conscience*, strict Presbyterians as to church-government. The toleration here described is entirely different from any thing known in Britain, or indeed at present thought of. The general sentiment even of those who claim not only the fullest toleration, but something beyond toleration, as their indisputable right, is, at least, "Separate places of worship for those of discordant opinions." The ground of the toleration here stated, likewise, is widely different from that which is at present insisted on; namely, that in matters of conscience towards God, no human authority has a right to interfere, provided nothing be avowed or done which threatens or disturbs the peace of the community; and that human authority can make only hypocrites, not willing and conscien-

monstrants went on to press this their toleration by every means, and to commend it privately and publicly in their writings and sermons; especially by this argument, that the articles, concerning which the controversy was maintained, they said, were of so small importance, that they did not relate to the ground or fundamental points of salvation; but in articles of this kind, toleration might and ought to be established.

July 25, 1614.] And thus they at length effected, that a decree concerning this toleration, some of the principal and powerful cities of Holland and West Friesland being unwilling and striving against it, should be published in print, confirmed with certain testimonies of Scripture and of the fathers (among whom they had also brought forward Faustus Regiensiensis, the leader of the Semi-Pelagians.) Against which things, when James Triglandius, a pastor of the church at Amsterdam, had answered in a public writing, Utenbogardus also prolixly attempted a defence of this decree. In this, he, by unworthy methods, traduced and reviled, as well the doctrine of the Reformed churches, as especially the lights of the same, Calvin, Beza, Zanchius, and others. To this writing, Triglandius opposed an accurate answer, in defence of the honour, both of the doctrine and the doctors of the Reformed churches. And when they (the Remonstrants) saw that the authority of this writing, to which they had given the name of a decree of the States, was

---

tious conformists. This is simple, intelligible, and evidently reasonable; but to tolerate *exclusively* opinions which do not relate to *the fundamentals of salvation*, or militate against them, must make way for intricate and endless disputes and difficulties, about what are and what are not the fundamentals of salvation; what is tolerated, and what is not tolerated.

not so great, as that by it they could attain to what they aimed at, they indicated that the same things must be attempted in another way; and for that purpose, a certain other formula of toleration having been devised in deceitful phrases, they, by the hands of certain persons, who secretly favoured their party and opinions, but were not considered as Remonstrants, solicited from the pastors subscription to this formula, every where throughout Holland, both privately and in their convention.

But when even in this way the business did not go on according to the purpose of their own mind; they judged, that those persons must be compelled (*cogendos*) by the authority of the superiors, whom they were not able to persuade to this, and that at length some time it must be broken through, and this business evidently accomplished. To this end they likewise obtained, that in the name of the illustrious, the States, the decree concerning mutual toleration, which had been published in the former year, should be sent to each of the Classes, and at the same time it should be enjoined on the pastors to obey the same without any contradiction. And that they might the more easily prefer those who were attached to their party, to the ministries of the churches, others having been excluded; they effected moreover that another (decree) should be joined to it, by which it was permitted, that in the vocation of pastors and elders it should be allowable to use that order, which in the year 1591 had been framed, but not approved; from the prescribed rule of which, the election was appointed to be by four of the magistracy, and four others to be deputed from the presbytery. When these decrees had been transmittod to the Classes, the most of them sent away their deputies to the illustrious, the States, that they might publicly explain their difficulties or grievances, which they had as to those things, that were contained in the writing, and might deprecate the introduction of the same. When on this account they had come to the Hague, and had now learned from the delegates of the principal cities, that those decrees, though they had already been transmitted, had not as yet been confirmed by the customary (*solemni*) approbation of all the States; and therefore could not as yet obtain the force of a law, they judged that they must desist from the design till they should be further pressed. But this last decree gave occasion to new contentions and disturbances in many places, especially in the church at Harlem. For when some magistrates determined that ministers should be called, according to this new form, and (thus) called them, but the churches did not approve it, it came to pass, that they refused to acknowledge those who had been thus called as their lawful pastors, and to have any ecclesiastical communion with them. It was also effected by these decrees, that certain Classes in Holland, which had hitherto preserved unity in the government of the churches, with the Remonstrants for the sake of peace, were now torn away from them (*divellerentur*), because the most of the pastors could not approve these things: yet as the Remonstrants purposed that the churches should be governed according to the prescript and law of these decrees, but were not able to extort this from their fellow ministers by authority, they introduced into the conventions of the Classes certain political persons, mostly alienated from the Reformed religion, and attached to their party, and brought dominion into the churches. For the orthodox pastors, tired out by the contentions which from these causes daily arose with the Remonstrants, judged it to be better to meet together apart without them, and to take care of their own churches in peace, than to be wearied with their perpetual contentions.

In the meantime Utenbogardus procured that it should be enjoined on his colleagues, by the authority of the superiors, to obey these decrees also; which when his colleague Henry Rosæus said that he could not promise with a good conscience, he was suspended from his office of teaching by the authority of the same persons, and by the sinister instigation of Utenbogardus.* Thence the members of the church at the Hague, who loved the purity (*sinceritatem*) of the Reformed doctrine, continued the exercise of their religion; at first indeed in the neighbouring village of Risverch, but when the pastors had obtained it by loan from the other churches at the Hague, in a separate place of worship (*templo*), to which afterwards some of the chief persons out of the States themselves, and the counsellors of the courts, and the other colleagues, and the most illustrious, the Prince of Orange himself, and the most Generous Count William Ludovicus, leaving the assemblies of the Remonstrants, resorted, that they might testify their consent to the orthodox doctrine, and their strong attachment to the same. The Remonstrants odiously traduced this separation under the title of SCHISM,† and endeavoured by all methods to hinder or to punish it: labouring in the meanwhile that these

* Whatever pretensions were made to toleration by the Remonstrants, it is from this most evident that they paid no due regard to the *rights of conscience*, the proper ground of all toleration.

† It commenced nearly as most other schisms have done; but all the blame did not rest on those stigmatized as *schismatics*, nor even the greatest measure of it.

decrees should be authoritatively put in execution in every place where they knew that the magistrate favoured them. On which account, when many pious men were punished by fines, prisons, and banishments, they appealed to the supreme tribunal of justice, and implored assistance against force; and when now the most ample, the Senators of the supreme court, attempted to succour the oppressed, they (the Remonstrants) obtained by the advocate of Holland, that an interdict should be laid on the same court, from protecting them.*

March, A. D. 1616.] But when many also and principal cities of Holland, and in the first place among them the most powerful city of Amsterdam, opposed the execution of these decrees, it was effected that Hugo Grotius with certain persons should be sent to Amsterdam, in order that by his eloquence he might persuade the most ample, the Senate of that city, to approve the same decrees. When he had attempted this with a prolix oration, it was answered by the most ample, the Senate, that they could by no means approve that, passing by the lawful synodical conventions, it should be deliberated in a convention of the States, concerning ecclesiastical affairs, that decrees should be made, and the execution of those decrees enjoined by authority; that it was purposed by them, that the true Christian religion, the exercise of which had flourished during fifty years in these regions, should be preserved; they judged also that even the least change

* What must the modern advocates for toleration, and more than toleration, think of that toleration which these men pleaded for, while thus employed in persecution; and who have rendered their opponents odious even to this day, as enemies to toleration, for rejecting their legal measures?

would be pernicious to the republic, unless it had been first maturely examined by a lawful Synod; and further, they could not assent to the different propositions and acts made from the year 1611, even to the eighteenth of March of this year, 1616, nor to this last proposition; neither were they willing that under the name of the city of Amsterdam, (when it was no feeble member of that convention of the States,) any decrees should be established, much less authoritatively carried into execution, or any thing decreed against those who professed the Reformed religion, unless controversies and changes in religion and in ecclesiastical affairs, had been first examined and discussed in lawful Synods, by the authority of the illustrious, the States. But neither were they willing that pastors who were attached to the opinion of the Reformed religion defended by the Contra-Remonstrants, should in the meantime on that account, either be suspended or removed from their ministerial offices, because they declared that they could not conscientiously cultivate ecclesiastical unity with the Remonstrants, neither that the churches which followed the same opinion should, under the pretext of *schism*, or because according to conscience they were reluctant to attend on the sermons of the Remonstrants, be hindered in the exercise of divine worship. And all these things they determined, until by the authority of the illustrious, the States, a lawful Synod should be convened, in which these controversies might be duly examined and discussed. Thus the labour and endeavour of the Remonstrants, and of those who favoured them, were in vain; especially because the magistrates of the most ample city of Dort, of Enckhuysen, of Edamen, and of Purmerent, publicly approved this determination of the Senate of Amsterdam.*

About this time, the pastors of Camp in Transylvania, having embraced the opinion of the Remonstrants, by the assistance of the magistracy, cast out of the ministry their most learned colleague, and most tenacious of sound doctrine, William Stephanus, because he opposed their attempts; and by pamphlets published, and by public sermons full of calumnies, they endeavoured to bring the Reformed religion into the hatred of the common people.

March, A. D. 1617.] When, on account of these innovations in doctrine, and the disturbances of the churches, and of the state which followed, they saw that they were rendered more and more odious, they presented a second Remonstrance to the States,† in which, with incredible impudence, they endeavoured to remove from themselves the crime of innovation, and to fasten the same on those pastors who most constantly remained in the received doctrine of these churches.‡ And the rest of the pastors presented likewise to the States a copious and solid answer

* As no intimation is here given of molesting the Remonstrants, either pastors or churches, but merely of preventing the Contra-Remonstrants from being molested till a Synod were held, this decision of the Senate of Amsterdam contains more of the spirit of toleration than any thing which we have yet met with.

[† Henceforth the titles of honour prefixed in the original to the States and individuals will be omitted.—*Editor of the Board of Publication.*]

‡ Either this whole narrative is false throughout, or this attempt was made with consummate effrontery; not indeed *incredible*, because other innovators, both ancient and modern, have endeavoured, and with success, to fasten the charge of innovation on those who most steadily abode by the doctrine of articles, &c., subscribed by all parties. But nothing is *incredible*, of which several undeniable instances may be adduced.

to it. But, whereas these long continued controversies had already brought not into the churches only, but the republic likewise, so great a mass of difficulties, perturbations, and confusions, that all who loved the safety of the federated provinces, or of the Reformed churches which are in them, or who favoured the same, understood that the remedy of these evils could no longer be deferred without the manifest danger of the state and of the churches; and yet the States had not been able hitherto to agree as to the kind of remedy: James I., out of his singular and sincere affection towards these regions and churches, thought that the States General should be admonished by letters, no longer to suffer this gangrene to feed upon the body of the republic: but that they should, as soon as possible, proceed to meet these unhappy contentions, divisions, schisms, and factions, which threatened manifest danger to the state. And at the same time he obtested them, that they would restore to its original purity, all errors having been extirpated, the true and ancient Reformed doctrine, which they had always professed, which had been confirmed by the common consent of all the Reformed churches, and which had been always the foundation and bond of that most strict friendship and conjunction, which had so long flourished between his kingdoms and these provinces; and which he judged might be done, of all means the most advantageously, by a national Synod, to be called together by their authority. For indeed this was the ordinary, legitimate, and most efficacious remedy, which had been had recourse to in every age, in evils of this kind among Christians. But moreover Maurice, prince of Orange, the governor of federated Belgium, as often before this, so now did not desist daily, in a most solemn and weighty manner, to obtest, as well the States General, and also the States of Holland and West Friesland, that in proportion as the safety of the republic and the churches was dear to them, so they would give diligent endeavours that a remedy, as soon as possible, might be applied to these most grievous evils. For this purpose he also commanded, and pressed upon them, the convocation of a national Synod, as the most ordinary and the safest remedy.

The States of Zealand also, by D. Malderæus, Brouwerus, Potterus, and Bonifiacius Junius, solemnly warned and entreated the orders of Holland and West Friesland, in their convention, that, seeing the contentions and dissensions grew more and more grievous every day, with the greatest danger of the republic, and many remedies had hitherto been tried in vain, that they would agree to the convoking of a national Synod, as the ordinary remedy proposed by the Holy Spirit for evils of this kind, and always had recourse to by Christians.* Then likewise the States of Gueldria, Friesland, Groningen, and Omland, requested the like thing by their deputies of the same States (General.)

* It has, I believe, been generally supposed, that the Synod of Dort was convened by a faction or party, and for party ends and purposes; but it seems undeniable, that it became the general and almost universal opinion of the different States in the confederated provinces, that such a national Synod as the Contra-Remonstrants always had urgently requested, was become absolutely and indispensably needful; and that the Remonstrants and their party could no longer resist this generally prevailing sentiment. Indeed, nothing can be more clear, than that all parties, except the zealous Remonstrants, regarded a national Synod as the proper and only effectual way of terminating the controversial disturbances; and not only sanctioned by the ex-

But when the Remonstrants saw that the convoking of a national Synod was recommended with so great earnestness by kings and princes, and the neighbouring and federated republics, yea, and also by the principal cities of Holland and West Friesland, and when they feared lest the States of Holland and West Friesland, of whom many of their own accord inclined to it, and promoted this business diligently, should at length be moved to this consent; and so, that at some time, an account must be rendered of their doctrine and actions before the ecclesiastical tribunals, in order to avoid this, they at first proposed a new way of settling the controversies, namely, that a few persons, both political and ecclesiastical, of a certain and equal number, should be chosen by the States of Holland and West Friesland, who, having communicated counsels with each other, might devise some method of peace and concord, which having been approved by the States, might then be prescribed to the churches. But when this did not succeed, (because the more prudent easily foresaw from whom, and of what kind of persons this convention would be constituted, and what was to be expected from it; and besides, that it was unprecedented in the churches, and very little suited for taking away ecclesiastical controversies in things pertaining to doctrine,) they thought that the most extreme measures must be tried, rather than be reduced to this necessity; and accordingly recourse was had to the most

---

ample of Christians in every age, but enjoined by God himself. How far they were warranted in this sentiment, constitutes a distinct question. The Synod of Dort, however, should not be judged by our modern opinions, but by the general opinion of that age. The reasons why the Remonstrants dissented from that opinion are very evident.

desperate counsels. For some of the chief persons (or nobles, *proceribus*) were persuaded by them that the calling of a national Synod, which was then pleaded for, was adverse to the majesty and liberty of the provinces; for that each province possessed the supreme right of determining about religion as it should seem good to it: that it was an unworthy thing to subject this their liberty to the judgment of other provinces; (and) that this right of majesty was to be defended by all means, even by arms. By these and similar arguments, the minds of the more imprudent were so stirred up that the rulers of some cities, having made a conspiracy, decreed to levy soldiers, who should be bound by oath, neither to the States General, nor to the Prince of Orange, the Commander-in-chief of the army, but to themselves alone, for the defence of the cause of the Remonstrants, and of their own authority; which for the sake of the same (cause) they had exposed to danger. This was done at Utrecht, in which city the States General had a garrison sufficiently strong against tumults and seditions; at Harlem, Leyden, Rotterdam, as also Gouda, Schookhove, Horn, and other places; the Remonstrants instigating the magistrates of the cities to this, as may be clearly proved by divers of their letters, which afterwards came into (the) hands (of the States.) And thus the dissensions of the Remonstrants would have brought these flourishing provinces into the danger of a civil war, if this madness had not been early repressed by the singular prudence of the States General, and by the vigilance and fortitude of mind, never to be sufficiently celebrated (*depredicanda*), of the Prince of Orange.*

* How far the subsequent proceedings against the Remonstrants are to be considered simply as religious persecution, may well be

The States General, when they saw that by this method the provinces were brought into extreme danger, judged that the calling of a national Synod must no longer be delayed, but be hastened at the earliest opportunity; especially when Dudley Carleton, the ambassador of the King of Great Britain, by a very weighty and prudent speech, had earnestly stirred up their Illustrious Highnesses to the same. This oration the Remonstrants afterwards were not afraid publicly to revile, in a most impudent and most calumniating pamphlet, to which they gave the title of *Bilancis;* sparing with a slanderous tongue no order of men, not the States, not the Prince of Orange, yea, not even the King of Great Britain. This pamphlet the States General condemned by a public edict as scandalous and seditious, having offered a most ample reward if any one could point out the author. Afterwards Jo. Casimirus Junius, the son of the most celebrated Francis Junius, not unlike his father, (*haud degener,*) copiously refuted the same. Therefore the States decreed the convoking of a national Synod, at length, in the name of the Lord, to be held on the first day of May in the following year; and at the same time they enacted some laws, according to which they willed as well that the convocation should be instituted, as the Synod itself held. But because the Remonstrants did not appear greatly to regard the judgment of the Belgic churches, and had always endeavoured to persuade the people that they did

---

questioned, when such seditious, if not treasonable practices, were proved against them from their own letters. It seems evident from this history that recourse to arms, in the first instance at least, was had by the party of the Remonstrants, and in opposition to existing laws. This is not generally understood. The rights of conscience, and the toleration arising from the recognition of it, seems to have been equally unthought of by both parties.

not dissent from the opinion of the Reformed churches, it seemed good, also, to invite from all the Reformed churches of the neighbouring kingdoms, principalities, and republics, some theologians, distinguished for piety, learning, and prudence, that they might support by their judgments and counsels the deputies of the Belgic churches; and that so these controversies, having been examined and thoroughly discussed, as it were, by the common judgment of all the Reformed churches, might be composed so much the more certainly, happily, safely, and with the greater benefit.

Dec. 11, 1617.] This decree having been made, the Remonstrants began in a wonderful manner to make disturbances, and proposed various other projects (*conceptibus*) by those who were attached to their cause, in endeavouring to overturn it and render it of no effect; in Holland, indeed, they themselves, by their favourers, demanded a provincial Synod, against which a little while ago they had entertained so strong an aversion (*tantopere abhorruerant*). And because measures had been devised for calling foreign theologians to the national Synod, they thought that to this provincial Synod, if so it seemed good, some foreign theologians might be (invited). But it was answered, that indeed a provincial Synod had formerly been demanded by the churches of Holland, when no hope appeared of obtaining a national Synod, and when the controversies were confined within the boundaries of the churches of Holland alone; but now, because the calling of a national Synod had been decreed, and the evil had diffused itself through all the provinces, so that it could not be taken away by the Synod of one province, it was at this time altogether unreasonable to think of a provincial Synod, for the composing of these controversies. Because, in like manner, as it behoved particular Synods in each of the provinces, to precede the national Synod, so in Holland also, both North and South (Holland), particular Synods would precede. Yet the Remonstrants, by their favourers, pressed eagerly and urged such a Synod: either because they thought that it would less obstruct their cause, as they had in Holland so many great men and even pastors favouring them; or that they might by this tergiversation absolutely hinder the calling of the national Synod. But when they themselves saw that this demand was too unjust for them easily to persuade (the granting of) it, they fled to a new exception, and desired (or proposed) that this cause should be deferred (or reserved) to a general council (*œcumenicam*). But it was answered them, that it was most uncertain whether or when a general council could be called; yet that these evils required a present remedy, and that this national (Synod) about to be called by the States General would be, as it were, an œcumenical and general (council); when deputies from almost all the Reformed churches would be present at the same. If they should account themselves aggrieved by the judgment of such a Synod, it would always be entire and lawful to them to appeal from this national to a general council; provided only, that in the meantime they obeyed the judgment of the national Synod. By these evasions and subterfuges they effected that the letters of convocation were for some little time delayed; and it was necessary that the day appointed for the meeting should be changed and deferred.*

* The conduct of the Remonstrants, on this occasion, evidently resembled that of an accused person who, instead of demanding a fair trial, objects to the authority of the court, challenges the jurymen,

In the mean while that most illustrious person, Dudley Carleton, in the convention of the States General, publicly complained that the honour of his master, the King of Great Britain, had been very unworthily and impudently reviled in the infamous libel (or pamphlet) *Bilancis*, which the Remonstrants, even after the edict of their Highnesses, had taken care should be printed again, having been translated into the French language; and having briefly and solidly refuted most of the objections of the Remonstrants, he explained to the States General what method the King of Great Britain was accustomed to employ in settling controversies concerning religion or doctrine, which, because it agreed with the decree of the States General, it more and more confirmed their Highnesses in this holy determination. The Magistracy also of the city of Amsterdam, having communicated counsel previously with the pastors of that church, and others called together for this cause, propounded in writing many and very weighty reasons, in the convention of the States of Holland and West Friesland, in which it was most evidently demonstrated that these controversies could not be determined at this season by any other method, than by a national Synod; at the same time they most solidly answered all the objections of the Remonstrants, and all their projects concerning a provincial Synod, and also concerning a general council. Soon after, likewise, the Magistracy of the city of Enckhuysen, having exhibited many reasons in writing also, approved the same. These reasons were afterwards made public, that

---

and endeavours to find out flaws in the indictment, and adopts every evasion to escape the trial, which can be suggested by his solicitor or counsel.

it might be evident to all men how unjustly the Remonstrants and their favourers acted, because they obstinately resisted the calling of a national Synod by these new projects, and eluded (*subterfugerent*) its decision.

The States General, as they judged that this thing so entirely necessary, and for the most just and weighty causes already decreed, was not to be any longer delayed on account of projects and shiftings of this kind, again decreed, that the convocation of a national Synod, without any delay or adjournment, should be immediately instituted; and they determine that the city Dordrecht (or Dort) should be the place of its meeting; the day, the first of the next November. When some persons among the States of Holland and West Friesland, favouring the cause of the Remonstrants, opposed themselves to this decree, in the convention of the States General, who complained that an injury was done to the majesty, the right, and finally, the liberty of that province, the States General declared by public letters, that they did not purpose by this convocation of a national Synod that any thing should be taken away from, or lessened in the majesty, right, or liberty of any province; but that this was the sincere intention of their Highnesses, that without any prejudice of any province, and even of the union and confederation, by the ordinary decision of a national Synod, the ecclesiastical controversies alone that had arisen concerning doctrine, which pertained to all the Reformed Belgic churches, should lawfully be determined to the glory of God, and the peace of the republic and of the churches. They then addressed letters to the States of each of the provinces, in which they declared that it had been determined by them to call together, in the name of the Lord, from all the churches of these provinces a national Synod on the first of November ensuing; that by this method the controversies which had arisen in the same churches, might be lawfully examined and settled in a beneficial manner, (truth being always preserved.)

At the same time they admonished them, that as soon as they could, they would call a provincial Synod in their own provinces, after the accustomed manner; from which six pious and learned men, and greatly loving peace, namely, three or four pastors, with two or three other proper persons, professing the Reformed religion, might be deputed, who, in the aforementioned national Synod, according to the laws constituted by them, (a copy of which they transmitted,) might examine those controversies and take them away, truth being preserved, (or safe, *salva veritate.*) To the Gallo-Belgic churches also (of French Flanders,) which used to constitute a peculiar Synod among themselves, seeing they had been dispersed through all these provinces, they addressed letters of the same kind. These letters having been received, the States of each of the provinces, called together the provincial or particular Synods of their own churches, in which the grievances might be proposed which were to be carried to the national Synod, the persons to be sent out to the same be deputed, and the commands with which these were to be furnished, framed by the common suffrages of the churches. These things were transacted in each of the piovinces, in the manner hitherto in use in these Reformed churches; except that in Holland and in the province of Utrecht, because of the very great number of the Remonstrants, the customary method could not in all things be observed. For when in Holland separations had been made in some of the Classes, so that the Remonstrants held their own Class-meetings apart, and the other pastors theirs also, it seemed proper to the States of that province, that of the Classes, in which a separation of this kind had not been made, four should be deputed by the majority of votes, in the manner hitherto customary, who with the ordinary power might be sent forth to the particular Synod; but in the other Classes, for the sake of avoiding confusion, the Remonstrants should appoint two, and the other pastors in like manner two, who might be sent with equal power to the particular Synod. In the province of Utrecht, the churches had not been distributed into certain Classes, wherefore it pleased the States of that province that all the Remonstrants should meet together apart in one Synod; but the rest of the pastors, who did not follow the opinion of the Remonstrants, of whom there still remained no small number, in another (Synod,) and that from each Synod and party three should be sent forth to the national Synod with the power of judging.

But the church of Utrecht, as it had been torn asunder into parties, of which the one followed the opinion of the Remonstrants, but the other disapproved of it; and this (party) recently set at liberty from the oppression of the Remonstrants, had not made provision for stated pastors, but used at that time the ministry of John Dipetzius, a pastor of Dort, it so happened that he was lawfully deputed by another Synod, in the name of the churches of Utrecht, which did not follow the opinion of the Remonstrants. But when the Synod of the churches of Gueldria and Zutphen had been assembled at Arnheim, the Remonstrant deputies from the Classis of Bommellien refused to sit along with the rest, unless previously certain conditions had been performed to them, which the Synod judged to be opposed to the decree of the States. And when ten articles had before this been offered by the Remonstrants of the Classis of Neomage, Bommelli and Tiel, to the States of Gueldria, and to the counsellors of the same, which they intimated to be taught by the rest of the pastors; it had been enjoined on them that they should publicly name those pastors who taught these things, in order that they might be cited before the Synod, that it might in a legal manner be examined, whether the matter were so indeed. For it was evident (*constabat*) that those articles had been framed by the Remonstrants in a calumniating manner, in order to excite odium (*ad conflandam invidiam*) against the rest of the pastors, before the supreme magistracy. But they were not able to name any one in that whole province, except the pastor of Hattemis, who had abundantly cleared himself to the Classis; and when the Synod nevertheless was willing to cite him, that he might be heard before them, the Remonstrants no further pressed it. Certainly, Henry Arnoldi, a pastor of Delft, who was present in the name of the churches of South Holland, declared that there was no one in South Holland who approved or taught these things.* Therefore the Synod severely reproved them for these atrocious

* In like manner it is at this day confidently asserted by writers, who, on one account or another, are regarded as worthy of credit, and thus it is generally believed that there are a numerous set of men in Britain, called Calvinists, or Methodists, or evangelical preachers, who preach doctrines, defined and stated by the writers, and justly deemed absurd and pernicious; who, if they were thus authoritatively called on to prove their assertions, would scarcely be able to substantiate the charge on one individual of the whole company.

calumnies; and at the same time declared, that the churches of Gueldria did not embrace or approve the doctrine contained in these articles, as it was set forth by them: though there were in them some sentences, which, taken apart, and in an accommodating sense, could not be disapproved. Then, at length, having confessed the crime of a calumny, into which they had been driven (*impactæ calumniæ*), they requested forgiveness of it (*eam deprecati sunt*). There was then drawn up in the same Synod, a state of the controversy between the Remonstrants and the rest of the pastors, which afterwards was exhibited to the national Synod. And as there were many pastors in that province, of whom some had been suspected of various other errors besides the five articles of the Remonstrants, others had illegally intruded into the ministry, and finally, others were of profligate life; some of them having been cited before the Synod, for these causes were suspended from the ministry, but by no means because of the opinion contained in the five articles of the Remonstrants, which were reserved to the national Synod. The cause of the rest, having been left in the name of the Synod, was referred to some persons deputed by it, to whom the States likewise joined their own delegates. These causes having been fully examined in their Classes, they suspended certain of them from their ministry, and others they entirely removed.

In the mean while the States General, when they had several times commanded those of Utrecht especially to dismiss the new soldiers, and those who, it appeared, had been levied for this purpose also, that the execution of the decrees of the future national Synod, if perhaps the Remonstrants could not approve of them, might be hindered by an armed force; determined that all these soldiers, of which there were now some thousands, should, as soon as possible, be disbanded and discharged by their authority. And when this measure had been carried into effect by the Prince of Orange, with incredible fortitude of soul, prudence, dexterity, and promptitude, without any effusion of blood, and their principal officers, who had endeavoured by force to resist this disbanding of them, had been committed to custody, John Utenbogardus, James Taurinus, and Adolphus Venator, conscious in themselves of criminality (*male sibi conscii*), having deserted their churches, fled out of federated Belgium, as likewise did a short time after Nicolas Grevinchovius, having been cited by the court of Holland to plead his own cause. And when a particular Synod in South Holland had been called at Delft, most of the Remonstrants, despising the before mentioned decree of the States, refused to depute any person to the Synod; and having presented a little suppliant book (*libello supplice*) to the States of Holland and West Friesland, they petitioned that, instead of the national Synod now proclaimed, another convention, instituted according to the same twelve conditions, which those who were cited afterwards laid before the national Synod, might be called. The States, having heard the judgment of the Synod of Delft, concerning this demand, (which also was inserted in these acts,) commanded them to obey the constituted order, and the mandates of the States; and moreover, fully to state their opinion comprised in writing, concerning the articles proposed in the conference at Delft, in the year 1613; and to add all their considerations, which they had respecting the Confession and Catechism of these churches. They exhibited the declaration of their opinion on the before mentioned articles, which afterwards, having been translated into Latin by the delegates of this Synod, was communicated to the national Synod: but, in the place of considerations, they sent some things gathered out of the writings of certain learned men, as if opposite to the Confession and the Catechism.

Before this Synod, John Utenbogardus and Nicolas Grevinchovius were cited; and when the former, as a fugitive (*profugus*), dared not to appear, but the latter contumaciously refused, the accusations produced against them having been examined, each of them was by the judgment of this Synod removed from the ecclesiastical ministry. But when in South Holland, besides these two, there were many others, of whom the most in these dissensions had been obtruded on unwilling churches without a lawful vocation; and others, who besides these five articles, had moreover scattered many Socinian errors, others had grievously offended the churches by wicked and turbulent actions, and others finally led a profane life; it was judged necessary, in order that the churches should be purified from these scandals, and the discipline of the clergy, as it is called, which had fallen into decay, should at length be restored, that all these disorderly (ἀτάκτους) pastors should be cited, that they might render before the Synod an account, as well of their vocation as of their doctrine, and also of their life; which seemed proper to be done even for this cause also, before the national Synod, that if perhaps any should deem themselves aggrieved by the sentence of the Synod or its deputies, they might appeal to the judgment (of the national Synod.) Certain of these appeared, whose causes having been duly examined, some of them were suspended from their office, and others wholly set aside. But as to those who, because of the shortness of the time, having been cited, could not be heard, and those who having been cited, had not appeared, five pastors were deputed, to whom the States joined also three deputies who might take cognizance of their cause, and give sentence upon it in the name of the Synod. But it was expressly enjoined on these deputies not to fix any censure on any one, because of the opinion expressed in the five articles of the Remonstrants, forasmuch as the judgment concerning the same had been reserved entire to the national Synod. But they, though they every where on the aforementioned most weighty causes, even during the national Synod, suspended many, partly from the office of teaching, and partly entirely set them aside; yet marked no one with any censure because of the opinion of the five articles, as it may be evidently shown from their very Acts.* In North Holland matters were conducted after the same method, in the Synod of Horn, in which the pastors of Horn, John Valesius, John Rodingenus, and Isaac Welsingius, having been suspended from the office of teaching, appealed to the national Synod. And when the deputies of this Synod, along with the delegates of the States, examined, in the Classis of Alcmar, the cause of John Geystran, a pastor of Alcmar, and of Peter Geystran, his brother, a pastor of Egmond, it was discovered that they had been evidently addicted to the blasphemous and execrable errors of Socinus,

* The appeal is thus made to the registered Acts of these deputies, evidently because they had been or were likely to be misrepresented by the favourers of the Remonstrants; as, beyond doubt, they generally have been to this very day.

as it appears from their own confession, which, because it was publicly read in the national Synod, to the horror of all men is likewise inserted in these Acts. In the Synod of the Transylvanian churches, some of the Remonstrants were commanded to render an account of their doctrine and actions; and when among them four pastors of the church of Campe, Thomas Goswin, Assuerus Matthisius, John Scotlerus, and above all, Everard Vosculius, had been accused of many errors, and of various turbulent actions, the cause having been examined, it seemed good to reserve it for the national Synod, even as it was afterwards brought before the same. In the other provinces, because no manifest Remonstrants were found, the Synods there held duly prepared all things with less labour, after the accustomed manner, for the national Synod.

In the mean time, the States General had addressed letters to James I., king of Great Britain, to the deputies of the Reformed churches of the kingdom of France, to the Elector Palatine, and the Elector of Brandenburg; to the Landgrave of Hesse; to the four reformed republics of Helvetia, (Switzerland,) Zurich, Berne, Basil and Schaffhausen, to the Counts of Correspondentia and Wedevarica; to the republics of Geneva, Bremen, and Emden, in which they requested, that they would deign to send from them to this Synod, some of their own theologians, excelling in learning, piety, and prudence, who might earnestly labour by their counsels and decisions, along with the rest of the deputies of the Belgic churches, to settle those controversies, which had arisen in these Belgic churches, and to restore peace to the same.

All these things having been duly prepared and completed, when at the appointed time as well the deputies of the Belgic churches, as also the foreign theologians, a few excepted, had met together at Dordrecht, (or Dort,) that national Synod was begun in the name of the Lord, on the thirteenth day of November (1618.) But in this Synod, what now was actually done, the prudent reader may copiously (*prolixè*) know from the Acts of the same, which now are published for the favour (satisfaction, *gratiam*) and use of the Reformed churches. It hath seemed good also, that to these Acts should be joined, besides other writings exhibited to this Synod, the judgments also of the theologians, concerning the five articles of the Remonstrants as they were proposed in the Synod; by which they may more fully know, by the same, on what passages of Scripture, and on what arguments, the canons of the Reformed church do rest. It is not to be doubted, but that the prudent reader will discover in these judgments, the highest and most admirable agreement. If perhaps in less matters a certain diversity appear, even this will be an argument, that a due liberty of prophesying and judging flourished in this venerable convention; but that all, notwithstanding, by concording opinions, agreed in the doctrine expressed in the canons of this Synod, of whom all and every one, (not one indeed excepted, or declining to do it,) subscribed to testify this consent.

But all the Reformed churches are requested willingly to embrace, preserve and propagate this orthodox doctrine, so solemnly in this Synod explained and confirmed from the word of God; and transmit it to all posterity, to the glory of divine grace, and the consolation and salvation of souls. And at the same time also favourably to receive the pious, and never sufficiently to be celebrated, zeal and earnest endeavour of the States General of federated Belgium, for preserving the purity (*sinceritate*) of the Reformed religion, and also to follow up with their favour, the diligence and piety in maintaining the same, of so many doctors of distinguished churches, who were present at this Synod; and, above all things, it is requested that they would earnestly entreat the most high and gracious God (*optimum maximum*) that he would indeed benignly preserve the Belgic churches, and in like manner all others professing with them the same orthodox doctrine, in the unity of the faith, in peace and tranquillity; and that he would inspire a better mind into the Remonstrants themselves, and all others who are involved in error;* and by the grace of his own Spirit, would at length some time lead them to the knowledge of the truth, to the glory of his own divine name, the edification of the churches, and the salvation of us all, through our Lord and Saviour Jesus Christ; to whom with the Father, and the Holy Spirit, the one, true, and immortal God, be praise, and honour, and glory, for ever and ever. Amen !†

* "That it may please thee to bring into the way of truth all such as have erred and are deceived."—(Litany.) The Calvinism of the Synod did not, it seems, prevent their prayers for those who, as they supposed, were in error. It did not lead them to treat their most eager opponents as *reprobates*, and give up as necessarily consigned to destruction, as many ignorantly suppose, or confidently assert that decided Calvinists do, even with malignity and malignant satisfaction. So greatly are they calumniated !

† "Accordingly a Synod was convoked at Dordrecht in the year 1618, by the counsels and influence of prince Maurice, &c."—(Mosheim, vol. v., p. 450). "Our author always forgets to mention the order issued by the States General for the convocation of this famous Synod; and by his manner of expressing himself, and particularly by the phrase (*Mauritio auctore*) would seem to insinuate, that it was by this prince that the assembly was called together. The legitimacy

of the manner of convoking this Synod was questioned by Olden-Barneveldt, who maintained that the States General had no sort of authority in matters of religion: affirming that this was an act of sovereignty that belonged to each province separately, and respectively."—(Maclaine, Ibid.)

It was by means of these disputes about the ecclesiastical authority (which all parties supposed to be possessed by some of them), that the union of the confederated States was endangered in this controversy.

"Dr. Mosheim, however impartial, seems to have consulted more the authors of one side than of the other, probably because they were more numerous, and more generally known. When he published this history, the world had not been favoured with *The Letters, Memoirs, and Negotiations* of Sir Dudley Carleton, which Lord Royston (afterwards Earl of Hardwicke) drew from his inestimable treasure of historical manuscripts, and presented to the public, or rather at first to a select number of persons, to whom he distributed a small number of copies, printed at his own expense. They were soon translated both into Dutch and French; and though it cannot be affirmed that the spirit of party is nowhere discoverable in them, yet they contain anecdotes with respect both to Olden-Barneveldt and Grotius, that the Arminians, and the other patrons of these two great men, have been studious to conceal. These anecdotes, though they may not be sufficient to justify the severities exercised against these eminent men, would, however, have prevented Dr. Mosheim from saying that he knew not on what pretext they were arrested." (Mosheim, vol. v., pp. 449, 450. Note by Maclaine.)

In a political contest for authority, between prince Maurice and his opponents, in the States General, the Remonstrants favoured his opponents, and the Contra-Remonstrants were attached to him. The prince's party at length prevailed, and "the men who sat at the helm of government were cast into prison. Olden-Barneveldt, a man of wisdom and gravity, whose hairs were grown grey in the service of his country, lost his life on the public scaffold, while Grotius and Hoogerberts were condemned to perpetual imprisonment; under what pretext, or in consequence of what accusations or crimes, is unknown to us."—(Mosheim, vol. v., pp. 448, 449.)

THE JUDGMENT

OF THE

NATIONAL SYNOD OF THE REFORMED BELGIC CHURCHES,

HELD AT DORT, IN THE YEARS OF OUR LORD, 1618, 1619;

AT WHICH VERY MANY THEOLOGIANS OF THE REFORMED CHURCHES OF GREAT BRITAIN, GERMANY, AND FRANCE, WERE PRESENT, CONCERNING THE FIVE HEADS OF DOCTRINE CONTROVERTED IN THE BELGIC CHURCHES.

(Published on the 5th of May, A. D. 1619.)

PREFACE.

In the name of our Lord and Saviour Jesus Christ. Amen.

Among very many comforts which our Lord and Saviour Jesus Christ hath given to his own church militant, in this calamitous pilgrimage, that which he left unto it when about to go away to his Father, into the heavenly sanctuary, saying, "I am with you at all times, even unto the end of the world," is deservedly celebrated. The truth of this most delightful promise shines forth in the church of all ages, which, whilst it has been besieged from the beginning, not only by the open violence of enemies, but also by the secret craftiness of seducers, truly if at any time the Lord had deprived it of the salutary guard of his own promised presence, had long since been either crushed by the power of tyrants, or seduced into destruction by the fraud of impostors.

But that good Shepherd, who most constantly loveth his flock, for which he laid down his life, hath always, most seasonably, and often by his own right hand stretched forth, most miraculously repressed the rage of persecutors; and hath also detected and dissipated the crooked ways of seducers and their fraudulent counsels, by both demonstrating himself to be most effectually present (*præsentissimum*) in his church. Of this thing an illustrious instruction (*documentum*) exists in the history of the pious emperors, kings, and princes, whom the Son of God hath excited so often for the assistance of his church, hath fired with the holy zeal of his house, and by their help hath not only repressed the furious rage (*furores*) of tyrants, but also hath procured to his church when conflicting with false teachers, in various ways adulterating religion, the remedies of holy Synods; in which the faithful servants of Christ, by united prayers, counsels, and labours, have valiantly stood for the church, and for the truth of God; have intrepidly opposed themselves against the "ministers of Satan, though transforming themselves into angels of light;" have taken away the seeds of errors and discords; have preserved the church in the concord of pure religion; and have transmitted the genuine (*sincerum*) worship of God uncorrupted to posterity. With a similar benefit our faithful Saviour hath, at this time, testified his own gracious presence with the Belgic church, by one means or other (*aliquam*) very much afflicted for many years. For this church, rescued by the powerful hand of God from the tyranny of the Roman antichrist, and the horrible idolatry of popery, (or the popedom, *papatus*,) and many times most miraculously preserved in the dangers of a long-continued war, and flourishing in the concord of true doctrine and discipline, to the praise of her God, to an admirable increase of the republic and the joy of the whole Reformed world, James Arminius and his followers, holding out the name of Remonstrants, by various errors old as well as new, at first covertly, and then openly assaulted (*tentarunt*), and while it was pertinaciously disturbed with scandalous dissensions and schisms, they had brought it into such extreme danger that unless the mercy of our Saviour had most opportunely interposed in behalf of his most flourishing church, they had at length consumed it with the horrible conflagration of discords and schisms.

But blessed be the Lord for ever, who, after he had hid his face for a moment from us, (who by many ways had provoked his wrath and indignation,) hath made it attested to the whole world, that he doth not forget his covenant, nor contemn the signs of his own people. For when scarcely any hope of a remedy, humanly speaking (*humanitus*), appeared, he inspired this mind into the States General of confederated Belgium, (see Ezra vii. 27, 28,) that with the counsel and direction of the Prince of Orange, they determined to go forth to meet these raging evils, by those legitimate means which have been sanctioned by the examples of the apostles themselves, and of the Christian church that followed them, during a long course of years, and which have before this been had recourse to (*usurpatæ*) in the Belgic church, with much fruit; and they called a Synod at Dordrecht by their own authority, out of all the provinces which they governed; having sought out towards it both the favour of James, king of Great Britain, and of illustrious Princes, Counts, and Republics, and having obtained also very many most grave theologians, that by common judgment of so many divines of the Reformed church, those dogmas of Arminius and of his followers might be decided on accurately, and by the word of God alone; that the true doctrine might be confirmed, and the false rejected; and that concord, peace, and tranquillity might, by the divine blessing, be restored to the Belgic churches. This is the benefit of God, in which the Belgic churches exult; and then humbly acknowledge and thankfully proclaim the compassions of their faithful Saviour. Therefore this venerable Synod, (after a previous appointment and observance of prayers and fasting, by the authority of the Supreme Magistracy in all the Belgic churches, to deprecate the wrath of God, and to implore his gracious assistance,) being met together in the name of the Lord at Dordrecht, fired with the love of God (*divini numinis*) and for the salvation of the church, and after having invoked the name of God, having bound itself by a sacred oath that it would take the Holy Scriptures alone as the rule of judgment, and engage in the examination (*cognitione*) and decision of this cause with a good and upright conscience, attempted diligently, with great patience, to induce the principal patrons of those dogmas, being cited before them, to explain more fully their opinion concerning the known five heads of doctrine, and the grounds (or reasons) of that opinion.

But when they rejected the decision of the Synod, and refused to answer to their interrogatories, in that manner which was equitable, and when neither the admonitions of the Synod, nor the mandates of the delegates of the States General, nor yet even the commands of the States General, availed any thing with them, (the Synod) was compelled, by the command of the same lords, to enter on another way, according to the custom received of old, in ancient Synods; and from writings, confessions, and declarations, partly before published, and partly even exhibited to this Synod, an examination of those five dogmas (or points of doctrine) was instituted. Which, when it was now completed, by the singular grace of God, with the greatest diligence, fidelity, and conscience (or conscientiousness), with the consent of all and every one, this Synod, for the glory of God, and that it might take counsel for the entireness (*integritate*) of the saving truth, and for the tranquillity of consciences, and for the peace and safety of the Belgic church, determined that the following judgment, by which both the true opinion, agreeing with the word of God, concerning the aforesaid five heads of doctrine is explained, and the false opinion, and that discordant with the word of God is rejected, should be promulgated.

On this preface, I would make a few remarks:

1. If the expectations which the persons constituting this Synod, and of those who were concerned in convening it, as to the useful tendency and beneficial effects of such assemblies, were indeed ill-grounded, and, of course, the measure improper, the fault was not exclusively theirs, but that of the age in which they lived, and indeed of almost all preceding ages. Not one of the Reformers, or of the princes who favoured the Reformation, can be named, who did not judge either a general council, or national councils or Synods of some kind, proper measures for promoting the cause of truth and holiness, and counteracting the progress of schism, heresy, and false doctrine, and in every place where the Reformation was established,

assemblies of the rulers and teachers of the church, under one form or other, were employed either in framing, or sanctioning, the articles of faith adopted in each church, and in regulating the several particulars respecting the doctrine to be preached, the worship to be performed by by those who constituted each church, and the terms of officiating as ministers in their respective societies. The system of independency and *individuality*, so to speak, either of separate congregations, or ministers, or Christians, without any such common bond of union or concert, had not then been thought of, at least in modern times. And at this day, while numbers suppose that they steer their course at a distance from the rocks which endangered the first Reformers, as well as the whole church in former ages, it may well be questioned whether they do not run into the opposite extreme. Solomon says, or God himself by him, "In the multitude of counsellors there is safety;" yet who does not know, that through the evil dispositions and selfish conduct of those who constitute the counsellors, and senates, and parliaments of different nations, such abuses often occur in them, as form a manifest exception to this general maxim? Yet who does not also see, that parliaments, and counsellors, and laws, are in themselves very desirable, and far preferable to every thing being settled by the sole will or caprice of every one who by any means obtains authority? or that every man should do that which is right in his own eyes, as when there was no king in Israel? The abuse alone is the evil, and to be guarded against; the thing itself is allowedly beneficial.

The apostles themselves, when consulted by Paul and Barnabas, did not settle the question proposed to them by their own direct authority, but "the apostles and elders came together for to consider of this matter." Acts xv. 6. It is evident that some, even in "that first *general* council," as it is very improperly called, had strong prejudices against the measure which was finally decided on; yet its decrees proved a blessing of no small magnitude to the churches of Christ, whether constituted of Jewish or Gentile converts. Now, a measure thus sanctioned cannot be *evil in itself*, though General Councils and Synods should have in *many* or *most* instances been productive of far greater evil than good. The fault lay in the motives, the corrupt passions and wrong state of mind and heart of those who convened, and of those who constituted them, (that is, in the abuse of the thing,) not in the thing itself.

The apostles by their own authority might have decreed the same things, and have said, "It seemed good to the Holy Ghost and to us, &c.;" but they were not led by the Spirit of inspiration to adopt this method; they did nothing by absolute authority; it does not appear that any thing directly miraculous, or of immediate revelation, concurred in their decision. It was the result of arguments drawn from facts, and from the holy Scriptures, under the teaching of the Holy Spirit, not materially differing from what uninspired men, of the same character and heavenly "wisdom, without partiality and without hypocrisy," might have formed, under the mere ordinary teaching and superintendence of the same Spirit. Now, it is not impossible for God to raise up elders and teachers, bearing this holy character, and endued with this heavenly wisdom, in other ages and nations, who, coming together to consider of those things which corrupt the doctrine, worship, and purity, or disturb the peace, of the church, may form and promulgate decisions, so evidently grounded on a fair interpretation of the sacred oracles, and so powerfully enforced by the character and influence of those concerned, as, by the divine blessing, may produce the most extensively beneficial effects.

General councils, so called, convened by the concurring authority of many princes and rulers, over rival nations, are not likely to come to any such scriptural decisions; and the history of general councils is certainly suited exceedingly to damp our expectations from them. But the history of the Reformation, both on the continent and in this land, produces many instances of conventions, under one name or other, in which the rulers and teachers of the church, under the countenance of princes who favoured the cause of truth and holiness, came to such decisions, in the most important matters, as proved very extensive and permanent benefits to mankind, and which could not have been expected without united deliberations and determinations of this kind. The ministers and members of the establishment, in this land, at least, must be allowed to think that this was the case, in the framing of our articles, liturgy, and homilies.

It is true that afterwards *convocations* became useless, or even worse than useless, and so sunk into disuse, but this was not until the spirit of wisdom and piety, which actuated our first Reformers, had most grievously declined, and made way for a political and party spirit, in the persons concerned. Thus the *abuse* of the measure, not the measure itself, must bear the blame.

2. I observe from this preface, that the members of the Synod of Dort, in the most solemn manner, and in the language at least of genuine piety, declare the awful obliga-

tions under which they brought themselves, to decide the controverted questions according to the holy Scriptures alone, and their full consciousness that they had discharged this obligation in an upright manner. The names annexed to their decisions certainly include among them a great proportion of the most able Protestant and Reformed theologians in Europe: and who can doubt the sincerity of these professions, when coming from such men as Bishops Davenant and Ward, and those with whom they thus cordially united? Prejudices, mistakes, and faults of many kinds may be supposed in them, but the candid and pious mind recoils from the idea that the whole was *direct and intended hypocrisy.*

In fact, I must give it as my opinion at least, that they did fulfil their solemn engagement, and must confess, that fewer things appear to me *unscriptural* in these articles than in almost any human composition which I have read upon the subject. Of course I expect that anti-Calvinists will judge otherwise, and even many Calvinists; yet surely every candid man will allow that they honestly meant thus to decide, and thought that they had thus decided.

It may also be seen, in the course of this work, that their doctrine accorded with the Belgic articles before in force among them, to which the Contra-Remonstrants had all along appealed.

3. I would observe, that they seem to have aimed at too much in their deliberations and decisions, not too much for an *ordinary controversial* publication, but too much for an *authoritative standard,* to be entirely received and adhered to by all the ministers of religion and teachers of youth in the Belgic churches. I should indeed say *far too much.* And here I again avow my conviction of

the superior wisdom bestowed on the compilers of our articles on the several points under consideration, in which, while nothing essential is omitted or feebly stated, a generality of language is observed, far more suitable to the design than the decrees of this Synod, and tending to preserve peace and harmony among all truly humble Christians, who do not in all respects see eye to eye, yet may "receive one another, but not to doubtful disputations;" whereas the very exactness and particularity into which, what I must judge, scriptural doctrine is branched out, and errors reprobated, powerfully counteracted the intended effect, and probably more than any thing else, or all other things combined, has brought on this Synod such decided, but unmerited, odium and reproach.

4. I would observe, that using the arm of the magistrate, and inflicting penalties on those who stood out against the decisions of the Synod, not being mentioned in the preface, will more properly be considered in another stage of our progress. But had the decrees been promulgated, and compliance with them demanded from all who acted as ministers of religion, or teachers of youth in the established seminaries of the Belgic church, with simply the *exclusion* from such stations of those who declined compliance, or violated their engagements to comply, while a toleration was granted, as at present in Britain, either to preach or teach in other places or schools, the terms might indeed have been considered as too strict, and requiring more than could reasonably be expected; but in other respects, it does not appear that the conduct of the Synod would have been blamable. For every body or company of professed Christians, down from established national churches to independent dissenting congregations,

prescribe terms of communion, or of officiating as ministers on those who desire *voluntarily* to join them, and exclude such as decline compliance.

How far the revenues in the Belgic churches could with any propriety have been shared, and any portion of them allotted to what we might call the dissenting teachers, I am not prepared to say. But as toleration (in this sense at least) was no part of the system at the Reformation in any country, the ancient revenues for religious purposes, as far as they were preserved for those uses, of course were allotted to the established ministers in the different churches. Neither *dissenters*, nor *provision* for dissenters, were thought of, and it would afterwards have been expecting too much in general, to suppose that they who found themselves in possession of these revenues would voluntarily share them with the dissentients, or that rulers would venture to compel them. Yet, if to a full toleration something had publicly been allotted towards the support of *peaceful* and *conscientious* dissenting teachers, it would, as it appears to me, at least have had a most powerful effect in diminishing acrimony, silencing objections, and promoting peace and love.

ARTICLES

OF

THE SYNOD OF DORT.

The Articles of the Synod of Dort, Heylin introduces in this manner:—"Because particular men may sometimes be mistaken in a public doctrine, and that the judgment of such men being collected by the hands of their enemies, may be unfaithfully related, we will next look on the conclusions of the Synod of Dort, which is to be conceived to have delivered the genuine sense of all the parties, as being a representative of all the Calvinian Churches of Europe, (except those of France,) some few divines of England being added to them. Of the calling and proceedings of this Synod we shall have occasion to speak further in the following chapter. At this time I shall only lay down the results thereof in the five controverted points (as I find them abbreviated by Dan. Tilenus) according to the heads before mentioned in summing up the doctrine of the Council of Trent." (Refutation of Calvinism, p. 566.)

A few things may here be noted.—Is it very probable that such decided anti-Calvinists as Heylin or Collier should be impartial in their account of this celebrated Synod? Is it to be supposed that there was no difference of sentiment among the persons of whom it was composed? Were four divines an adequate representation of all the Calvinists in England? Did not one or more of all these four dissent from the decisions of this Synod? Were other Protestant countries represented in any great degree more adequately? Were not the leading men greatly embittered with personal enmities, and the spirit of persecution and resentment? Did not political interests and the spirit of party still more embitter the spirits, or sway the deliberations and conclusions of the Synod? And therefore are all the Calvinists who lived at that time, or who now live, or whoever shall live, to be judged according to the proceedings of the Synod of Dort? It would be no difficult undertaking by such a procedure to fix very heavy charges on the whole body of anti-Calvinists in Europe and in the world; but attempts of this kind prove nothing, except a disposition to act the part of a special pleader in the controversy, rather than that of an impartial judge. As I, however, had met with the same abstract of the articles of this Synod in other publications more favourable to Calvinism, I had no suspicion that these were not the real articles of the Synod, but an abbreviation, (yet with several clauses also *added*,) an abbreviation by avowed opponents. But the Christian Observer first excited a suspicion that these were not the real articles of the Synod, and led me to inquire after a copy of those articles, which are indeed immensely more discordant with the abbreviations than I could have previously imagined. But let the attentive reader judge from the following literal translation of these articles, &c. as contained in the *Sylloge Confessionum*, Oxford, 1804.

CHAPTER I.

OF THE DOCTRINE OF DIVINE PREDESTINATION.

ART. 1. As all men have sinned in Adam, and have become exposed to the curse and eternal death, God would have done no injustice to any one, if he had determined to leave the whole human race under sin and the curse, and to condemn them on account of sin; according to those words of the apostle, "All the world is become guilty before God." Rom. iii. 19. "All have sinned, and come short of the glory of God." verse 23. And, "The wages of sin is death." Rom. vi. 23.*

2. But "in this is the love of God manifested, that he sent his only-begotten Son into the world, that every one who believeth in him should not perish, but have everlasting life." 1 John iv. 9. John iii. 16.

3. But that men may be brought to faith, God mercifully sends heralds of this most joyful message, to whom he willeth, and when he willeth, by whose ministry men are called to repentance, and faith in Christ crucified. For "how shall they believe in him of whom they have not heard? and how shall they hear without a preacher? and how shall they preach except they be sent?" Rom. x. 14, 15.

4. They who believe not the Gospel, on them the wrath of God remaineth; but those who receive it, and embrace the Saviour Jesus with a true and living faith, are through

* Gal. iii. 10 22.—"In every person born into the world, it, (original sin,) deserveth God's wrath and damnation." Art. ix.

him, delivered from the wrath of God, and receive the gift of everlasting life (*ac vitâ æternâ donantur*). Rom. vi. 23.

5. The cause or fault of this unbelief, as also of other sins, is by no means in God, but in man. But faith in Jesus Christ, and salvation by him, is the free gift of God. "By grace are ye saved, through faith, and that not of yourselves, it is the gift of God." Eph. ii. 8. In like manner, "It is given you to believe in Christ." Phil. i. 29. (See Art. x.)

6. That some, *in time*, have faith given them by God, and others have it not given, proceeds from his *eternal* decree; for "known unto God are all his works, from the beginning of the world." Acts xv. 18. Eph. i. 11.* According to which decree, he graciously softens the hearts of the elect, however hard, and he bends them to believe; but the non-elect he leaves, in just judgment, to their own perversity and hardness.† And here, especially, a deep discrimination, at the same time both merciful and just, a discrimination of men equally lost, opens itself to us; or that decree of Election and Reprobation which is revealed in the word of God. Which, as perverse, impure, and unstable persons do wrest to their own destruc-

* Eph. i. 4, 5; iii. 11. 2 Thess. ii. 13, 14. 2 Tim. i. 9, 10. Tit. i. 2. 1 Pet. i. 2, 20. Rev. xiii. 8; xvii. 8.

† "Predestination to life is the everlasting purpose of God, whereby, before the foundations of the world were laid, he hath constantly decreed by his counsel, secret to us, to deliver from curse and damnation those whom he hath chosen in Christ out of mankind, and to bring them by Christ to everlasting salvation, as vessels made to honour. Wherefore, they which are endued with so excellent a benefit of God, be called according to God's purpose by his Spirit working in due season; they through grace obey the calling; they be justified freely, &c." Art. xvii.

tion, so it affords ineffable consolation to holy and pious souls.*

7. But Election is the immutable purpose of God, by which, before the foundations of the world were laid, he chose, out of the whole human race, fallen by their own fault from their primeval integrity into sin and destruction, according to the most free good pleasure of his own will, and of mere grace, a certain number of men, neither better nor worthier than others, but lying in the same misery with the rest, to salvation in Christ, whom he had, even from eternity, constituted Mediator and Head of all the elect, and the foundation of Salvation; and therefore he decreed to give them unto him to be saved, and effectually to call and draw them into communion with him, by his own word and Spirit; or he decreed himself to give unto them true faith,† to justify, to sanctify, and at length powerfully to glorify them, having been

* "As the godly consideration of predestination and our election in Christ is full of sweet, pleasant, and unspeakable comfort to godly persons, and such as feel in themselves the working of the Spirit of Christ, mortifying the works of the flesh and their earthly members, and drawing up their minds to high and heavenly things; as well because it doth greatly establish and confirm their faith of eternal salvation, to be enjoyed through Christ, as because it doth fervently kindle their love to God; so for curious and carnal persons, lacking the Spirit of Christ, to have continually before their eyes the sentence of God's predestination, is a most dangerous downfall, whereby the devil doth thrust them either into desperation, or into wretchlessness of most unclean living, no less perilous than desperation." Art. xvii. Whatever method of interpretation be adopted, as to the different parts of this our article, they who cordially approve it cannot consistently object to this article of the Synod of Dort, which is entirely coincident with it, and at least not more decided and explicit.

† "We believe that the Holy Spirit, dwelling in our hearts, imparts to us true faith, that we may obtain the knowledge of so great a mystery."—*Belgic Confession.*

kept in the communion of his Son, to the demonstration of his mercy, and the praise of the riches of his glorious grace, as it is written: "God hath chosen us in Christ before the foundations of the world were laid, that we should be holy and without blame before him in love, having predestinated us unto the adoption of children, by Jesus Christ to himself, according to the good pleasure of his will; to the praise of the glory of his grace, wherein he hath freely made us accepted to himself in that Beloved One." Eph. i. 4—6. And in another place, "Whom he did predestinate, them he also called; and whom he called, them he also justified; and whom he justified, them he also glorified." Rom. viii. 30.

8. This election is not multiform, but one and the same of all that shall be saved, in the Old and New Testament, seeing that the Scripture declares the good pleasure, purpose, and counsel of the will of God, by which he has, from eternity, chosen us to grace and glory: both to salvation and the way of salvation, which he hath "before prepared that we should walk in it." 2 Thess. ii. 13, 14. 1 Pet. i. 2.

9. This same election is not made from any foreseen faith, obedience of faith, holiness, or any other good quality and disposition, as a *prerequisite cause* or condition in the man who should be elected, but *unto* faith, and *unto* the obedience of faith, holiness, &c. And, therefore, (or truly, *proinde*,) election is the fountain of every saving benefit; whence faith, holiness, and the other salutary gifts, and finally, eternal life itself, flow as its fruit and effect, according to that word of the apostle: "He hath chosen us (not because we *were*, but) that we *might be* holy, and without blame before him in love." Eph. i. 4.

10. Now the cause of this gratuitous election is the sole good pleasure of God, (Matt. xi. 26. Eph. i. 5. 1 Tim. i. 9. James i. 18,) not consisting in this, that he elected into the condition of salvation certain qualities or human actions from all that were possible; but in that, out of the common multitude of sinners, he took to himself certain persons as his peculiar property, according to the Scripture: "For the *children* being not yet born, neither having done any good or evil, &c., it is said," (that is, to Rebecca,) "the elder shall serve the younger; even as it is written, Jacob have I loved, but Esau have I hated." Rom. ix. 11—13. And "as many as were ordained (*ordinati*) to eternal life, believed." Acts xiii. 48.

11. And as God himself is most wise, immutable, omniscient, and omnipotent, so election made by him can neither be interrupted, changed, recalled, nor broken off; nor can the elect be cast away, nor the number of them be diminished.

12. Of this, his eternal and immutable election to salvation, the elect, though by various steps, and in an unequal measure, are rendered certain (or assured), not indeed by curiously scrutinizing the deep and mysterious things of God, but by observing in themselves, with spiritual delight and holy pleasure, the infallible fruits of election described in God's word, such as true faith in Christ, filial fear of God, sorrow for sin, according unto God (λύπη κατὰ Θεὸν—"Godly sorrow,") (2 Cor. vii. 10 Gr.) hungering and thirsting after righteousness, &c.*

* How different is this from the generally circulated opinion, that they who believe election in the Calvinistic sense, are taught to assume it a certainty that they are the elect without further evidence! In this the vehement opposers, and the perverters of the doctrine, seem to coincide, but no more with the Synod of Dort, than with Peter's exhortation. 2 Pet. i. 5—10.

13. From the sense and assurance (*certitudine*) of this election, the children of God daily find greater cause of humbling themselves before God, of adoring the abyss of his mercies, of purifying themselves, and of more ardently loving him reciprocally who had before so loved them; so far are they from being rendered by this doctrine of election, and the meditation of it, more slothful in observing the divine commands, or carnally secure.* Wherefore, by the just judgment of God, it is wont to happen to those who either are rashly presuming, or idly and frowardly *prating* (*fabulantes*) about the grace of election, that they are not willing to walk in the ways of the elect.

14. But as this doctrine of divine election, in the most wise counsel of God, was predicated by the prophets, by Christ himself, and by the apostles, under the Old as well as under the New Testament, and then committed to the monuments of the sacred Scriptures, so it is to be declared at this day by the church of God, to whom it is peculiarly destinated, with a spirit of discrimination, in a holy and religious manner, in its own place and time, all curious scrutinizing the ways of the Most High being laid aside; and this to the glory of the most holy divine name, and for the lively solace of his people.†

15. Moreover, holy Scripture doth illustrate and commend to us this eternal and free grace of our election, in

---

* 1 Cor. xv. 58. Col. iii. 13, 14. 1 John iii. 2, 3.

† Election, as a part of divine revelation, and of the "whole counsel of God," must be preached; we must "not shun to declare it," for in doing so, what do we but presume ourselves wiser than He who revealed it as a part of his counsel, and decide that it ought not to have been revealed? But this declaration must be made with "discrimination, in a holy and religious manner, &c." Thus declared in its proper connection, application, and *proportion*, as in

this more especially, that it doth also testify all men not to be elected, but that some are non-elect, or *passed by* in the eternal election of God, whom truly God, from most free, just, irreprehensible, and immutable good pleasure, decreed to leave in the *common misery*, into which they had, by *their owu fault*, cast themselves, and not to bestow on them living faith, and the grace of conversion; but having been left in their own ways, and under just judgment, at length, not only on account of their unbelief, but also of all their other sins, to condemn and eternally punish them, to the manifestation of his own justice.* And this is the decree of reprobation, which determines that God is in no wise the author of sin, (which to be thought of is blasphemy,) but a tremendous, irreprehensible, just Judge and Avenger.

16. Those who do not as yet feel efficaciously in themselves a lively faith in Christ, or an assured confidence of

---

the sacred Scriptures, it will greatly conduce to improve the true believer's character, his humility, gratitude, admiring love of God, meekness, compassion, and good will to man, as well as his comfort and joy of hope. It will also exhibit the gospel of most free and rich grace in its unclouded glory, cast a clearer light on every other part of divine truth, and secure to the Lord alone the whole honour of man's salvation. Yet the same doctrine, rashly, indiscriminately, and disproportionately preached, and not properly stated and improved, does immense mischief.

* "He" (God) "secluded from saving grace all the rest of mankind (*except a very small number*), and appointed them by the same decree to eternal damnation, *without any regard to their infidelity and impenitency*."—Heylin's Abbreviation. Is not this a direct violation of the command, "Thou shalt not bear false witness against thy neighbour?" Or are not Calvinists to be considered as *neighbours* by anti-Calvinists? And do not they who retail the false accusation, *intentionally* or *heedlessly*, share a measure of the criminality? Is this the *moral practice* which is contended for by anti-Calvinists?

heart, peace of conscience, earnest desire (*studium*) of filial obedience, glorying in God through Christ, yet nevertheless use the means by which God has promised to work these things in us, ought not to be alarmed by the mention of reprobation, nor reckon themselves to be reprobate; but to use diligently the means of grace, and ardently to desire, and reverently and humbly to expect, the period of more abounding (or fructifying, *uberius*,) grace. And much less should those persons be terrified by the doctrine of reprobation, who, when seriously converted to God, simply desire to please him, and to be delivered from the body of death, yet cannot attain to what they wish in the path of faith and piety, because the merciful God hath promised that he will not "quench the smoking flax, nor break the bruised reed."* But this doctrine is justly for a terror to those who, forgetful of God and the Saviour Jesus Christ, have delivered themselves wholly to the cares and carnal pleasures of the world, so long as they are not in earnest (*serio*) converted unto God.

17. Seeing that we are to judge of the will of God by his word, which testifies that the children of believers are holy, not indeed by nature, but by the benefit of the gracious covenant, in which they are comprehended along with their parents, pious parents ought not to doubt of the election and salvation of their children, whom God hath called in infancy out of this life.†

* "Furthermore, we must receive God's promises, in such wise as they be generally set forth to us in holy Scripture, and that will of God is to be followed which we have expressly declared to us in the word of God."—Art. xvii. Church of England. John vi. 37—40.

† The salvation of the offspring of believers, dying in infancy, is here scripturally stated, and not limited to such as are baptized.

18. Against those who murmur at this grace of *gratuitous* election, and the severity of *just* reprobation, we oppose this word of the apostle, "O man, who art thou that repliest against God?" Rom. ix. 20; and that of our Saviour, "Is it not lawful for me to do what I will with mine own?" Matt. xx. 15. We, indeed, piously adoring these mysteries, exclaim with the apostle, "Oh, the depths of the riches, both of the wisdom and knowledge of God! How unsearchable are his judgments, and his ways past finding out! For who hath known the mind of the Lord, or who hath been his counsellor? Or who hath first given to him, and it shall be recompensed to him again? For of him, and through him, and to him, are all things; to whom be glory, for ever. Amen."*

These eighteen articles concerning predestination are *abbreviated* by Dan. Tilenus, and reported by Heylin, in the following single article:

OF DIVINE PREDESTINATION.

"That God, by an absolute decree, hath elected to salvation *a very small number* of men, without any regard to their faith and obedience whatsoever; and secluded from saving grace all the rest of mankind, and appointed them by the same decree to eternal damnation, without any regard to their infidelity and impenitency."

Nothing is said of the children of unbelievers dying in infancy, and the Scripture says nothing. But why might not these Calvinists have as favourable a hope of all infants dying before actual sin as anti-Calvinists can have?

* A more appropriate and scriptural conclusion of these articles cannot even be imagined.

I have long been aware that there is "no new thing under the sun," (Ecc. i. 9, 10,) and that "speaking all manner of evil falsely," of the disciples of Christ, is no exception to this rule; and that misrepresenting and slandering men called Calvinists has been very general ever since the term was invented; but I own I never before met with so gross, so barefaced, and inexcusable a misrepresentation as this, in all my studies of modern controversy. It can only be equalled by the false testimony borne against Jesus and his apostles, as recorded in holy writ. But is that cause likely to be in itself *good*, and of God, which needs to be supported by so unhallowed weapons?

REJECTION OF ERRORS BY WHICH THE BELGIC CHURCHES HAVE FOR SOME TIME BEEN DISTURBED.

The orthodox doctrine of election and reprobation having been stated, the Synod rejects the errors of those,

1. Who teach that "the will of God, concerning the saving of those who shall believe, and persevere in faith and the obedience of faith, is the whole and entire decree of election unto salvation, and that there is nothing else whatever concerning this decree revealed in the word of God." For these persons impose upon the more simple, and manifestly contradict the sacred Scripture, which testifies, not only that God will save those who shall believe, but also that he hath chosen certain persons from eternity, to whom, in preference to others (*præ aliis*), he may, in time, give faith and perseverance, as it is written, "I have made known thy name unto the men whom thou hast given me." John xvii. 6. Also, "As many as were ordained unto eternal life believed." Acts xiii 48. And,

"He hath chosen us before the foundation of the world, that we should be holy, &c." Eph. i. 4.

2. Who teach that "the election of God to eternal life is of different kinds (*multiplicem*); one, general and indefinite; another, singular and definite: and again, this either incomplete, revocable, not peremptory, or conditional; or else complete, irrevocable, peremptory or absolute." In like manner, "that one election is to faith, another to salvation; so that there may be an election to justifying faith, without a peremptory election to salvation." This is indeed a comment excogitated by the human brain without the Scriptures, corrupting the doctrine of election, and dissolving this golden chain of salvation. "Whom he predestinated, them he also called, whom he called, them he also justified, and whom he justified, them he also glorified." Rom. viii. 30.*

3. Who teach "that the good pleasure and purpose of God, which the Scripture mentions in the doctrine of election, does not consist in this, that God before selected certain men above the rest (*præ aliis*); but in this, that God chose, that from among all possible conditions, (among which are also the works of the law,) or from the order of all things, the act of faith, ignoble in itself, and the imperfect obedience of faith, should be the condition of salvation; and willed (*voluerit*) graciously to account this instead of perfect obedience, and to judge it of the

---

* They be called according to God's purpose by his Spirit working in due season; they through grace obey the calling, they be justified freely, they be made the children of God by adoption, they be made like the image of the only begotten Son, Jesus Christ, they walk religiously in good works, and at length by God's mercy they attain to everlasting felicity."—Art. xvii.

reward of eternal life. For by this pernicious error, the good pleasure of God and the merit of Christ are enervated, and men are called away by unprofitable disputations, from the truth of gratuitous justification and the simplicity of the Scriptures; and that of the apostle is accused of falsehood, "God hath called us with a holy calling, not of works, but of his own purpose and grace, which was given us in Christ Jesus, before the world began." 2 Tim. i. 9.*

4. Who teach that "in election to faith this condition is prerequired, that man should rightly use the light of nature; that he should be honest, lowly, humble, and disposed for eternal life, as if upon these things, in some measure, may election depend." For they savour of Pelagius, and by no means obscurely accuse the apostle of falsehood in writing, "Among whom we also had our conversation in times past, in the lusts of the flesh, fulfilling the desires of the flesh and of the mind, and were by nature the children of wrath, even as others. But God, who is rich in mercy, for his great love wherewith he loved us, even when we were dead in sins, hath made us alive together with Christ, (by grace ye are saved); and hath

* We are accounted righteous before God only for the merit of our Lord and Saviour Jesus Christ, by faith, and not for our own works or deservings."—Art. xi. "Faith is the only hand which putteth on Christ unto justification, and Christ the only garment which, being so put on, covereth the shame of our defiled nature, hideth the imperfection of our works, preserveth us blameless in the sight of God, before whom otherwise the weakness of our faith were cause sufficient to make us culpable: yea, to shut us from the kingdom of heaven, where nothing that is not absolute can enter."—Hooker. The error refuted in this article, is as contrary to the doctrine of our church as to that of the Synod of Dort.

raised us up together in heavenly places in Christ Jesus, that in the ages to come he might show the exceeding riches of his grace, in his kindness towards us through Christ Jesus. For by grace are ye saved, through faith, and that not of yourselves; it is the gift of God, not of works, lest any man should boast." Eph. ii. 3—9.*

5. Who teach that "election of individuals to salvation, incomplete and not peremptory, is made from foreseen faith, repentance and sanctity, and piety begun, and for some time persevered in; but that complete and peremptory election is from the foreseen final perseverance of faith, repentance, holiness and piety; and that this is the gracious and evangelical worthiness, on account of which he who is elected is more deserving than he who is not elected; and therefore, faith, the obedience of faith, holiness, piety, and perseverance, are not the fruits or effects of immutable election to glory, but the conditions and causes required beforehand, and foreseen as if they were performed in the persons to be elected, without which there cannot be complete election." This is what opposes the whole Scripture, which every where assails (*ingerit*) our ears and hearts with these and other sayings: Election is not of works, but of him that calleth. Rom. ix. 11. "As many as were ordained to eternal life, believed." Acts xiii. 48. "He chose us to himself, that we might be holy." Eph. i. 4. "Ye have not chosen me, but I have chosen you." John xv. 16. "If it is of grace, it is not of works." Rom. xi. 6. "Herein is love; not

* This error requires from unregenerate man, and ascribes to nature, that which is the effect of regeneration and grace. Prov. xvi. 1. James i. 15—17. Second Collect, Evening Service.

that we loved God, but that he loved us, and sent his own Son." 1 John iv. 10.*

6. Who teach that "not all election to salvation is immutable, but that some elect persons, no decree of God preventing (*obstante*), may perish, and do perish eternally." By which gross error they make God mutable, subvert the consolation of the godly concerning the stability of their election, and contradict the sacred Scriptures, whereby we are taught that the elect cannot be deceived (Matt. xxiv. 4); that "Christ loses not those who were given to him by the Father." John vi. 39. That "those whom he (God) hath predestinated, called, and justified, them he also glorifies." Rom. viii. 30.†

7. Who teach that "in this life there is no fruit, no sense, no certainty of immutable election to glory, except from a mutable and contingent condition." But, besides that it is absurd to mention an uncertain certainty, (*ponere incertam certitudinem*,) these things are opposite to the experience of the saints, who, with the apostle, exult in the consciousness of their election, and celebrate this benefit of God; who *rejoice* with the disciples, according to Christ's admonition, "that their names are written in heaven." Luke x. 20. Who finally oppose the feeling of election to the fiery darts of diabolical temptations, inquiring, "Who shall lay anything to the charge of God's elect." Rom. viii. 33.‡

---

* Some of the texts here adduced seem not decidedly conclusive, but may be otherwise explained; but others might easily be substituted. Eph. ii. 4, 5, 9, 10. 2 Tim. i. 9. James i. 17, 18. 1 Pet. i. 2.

† John x. 27—30. 2 Thess. ii. 13, 14. 1 Pet. i. 5, 23—25. 1 John iii. 9; v. 18.

‡ See Article xii. on Predestination.—"The godly consideration of predestination and our election in Christ is full of sweet, pleasant,

8. Who teach that "God has not decreed from his own mere just will, to leave any in the fall of Adam, and in the common state of sin and damnation, or to pass them by in the communication of grace necessary to faith and conversion." For that passage stands firm, "He hath mercy on whom he will have mercy, and whom he will he hardeneth." Rom. ix. 18. Also, "I glorify thee, O Father, Lord of heaven and earth, for that thou hast hid these things from the wise and prudent, and hast revealed them unto babes; even so, Father, for so it hath pleased thee." Matt. xi. 25, 26.

9. Who teach that "the reason why God sends the gospel to one nation rather than another is not the mere and sole good pleasure of God; but because this nation is better and more deserving than that to which the gospel is not communicated." Yet Moses recalls the people of Israel from this, saying, "Behold the heavens and the heaven of heavens is the Lord thy God's; the earth also, with all that therein is; only the Lord had a delight in thy fathers to love them; and he chose their seed after them, even you, above all people, as it is this day." Deut. x. 14, 15. And Christ, "Woe unto thee, Chorazin! Woe unto thee, Bethsaida! for if the mighty works that are done in thee, had been done in Tyre and Sidon, they

---

and unspeakable comfort to godly persons; and such as *feel in themselves* the working of the Spirit of Christ, mortifying the works of the flesh, and their earthly members, and drawing up their minds to high and heavenly things; as well because it doth greatly establish and confirm their faith of eternal salvation, to be enjoyed through Christ, as because it doth fervently kindle their love towards God." Art. xvii. of the Church of England.

would have repented long ago in sackcloth and ashes." Matt. xi. 21.*

"That we thus think and judge, we testify by the subscription of our hands."

Then follows a list of the names of all those who subscribed and attested these articles and refutations, among whom are found, George, Bishop of Llandaff, John Davenant, Presbyter, Doctor, and public professor of sacred theology in the University of Cambridge, and at the same time president (*præses*) of King's College. Samuel Ward, presbyter, Archdeacon of Taunton, Doctor of sacred theology, and head of Sidney College of the University of Cambridge Thomas Goad, presbyter, Doctor of sacred theology, and precentor of the cathedral church of St. Paul, London. Walter Balcanqual (*Scoto-Britannus*), a Scotchman, presbyter, Bachelor of sacred theology; with very many others from various parts of the continent of Europe, amounting to above eighty. These were deputed by churches, differing from each other in various respects, Episcopalians, Presbyterians, and those in some of the regions which are generally accounted Lutheran, and men that occupied the most important stations in the church and universities of their several countries; yet they all subscribed these articles of the Synod, agreeing in this respect though not in others. For it cannot be supposed that they who opposed, or were much dissatisfied with any of the conclusions, would thus *voluntarily and solemnly attest and subscribe* the same decisions. This consideration should, in all reason, at least, induce us to give these articles a candid and attentive

* This shows that the election of nations is really as opposite to the anti-Calvinist's ideas of divine justice as the election of individuals.

examination, comparing them carefully with the Scriptures of truth, and praying for the teaching of the Holy Spirit, that we may not be so left "to lean to our own understanding," as to *reject* and even to *revile* that which perhaps may, in great part at least, accord with the "sure testimony of God."

CHAPTER II.

ON THE DOCTRINE OF THE DEATH OF CHRIST, AND THROUGH IT THE REDEMPTION OF MEN.

1. God is not only supremely merciful, but also supremely just. And his justice requires, (according as he hath revealed himself in the word,) that our sins committed against his infinite majesty, should be punished not only with temporal, but also with eternal sufferings—of soul as well as of body; which punishment we cannot escape, unless the justice of God be satisfied. Isa. xlv. 21. Rom. iii. 25, 26.

2. But as we cannot satisfy it, and deliver ourselves from the wrath of God, God of infinite mercy gave to us his only begotten Son as a surety, who, that he might make satisfaction for us, was made sin and a curse on the cross for us, or in our stead.*

3. This death of the Son of God is a single and most perfect sacrifice and satisfaction for sins, of infinite value and price, abundantly sufficient to expiate the sins of the whole world.†

* Isa. liii. 4—6, 10, 11. 2 Cor. v. 21. Gal. iii. 13. 1 Pet. ii. 24; iii. 18.

† John i. 29. 1 John ii. 2. Prayer of consecration, Communion Service. Catechism, second instruction from the articles of the creed.

4. But this death is of so much value and price on this account, because the person who endured it is not only truly and perfectly a holy man, but also the only begotten Son of God, of the same eternal and infinite essence with God the Father and the Holy Spirit, such as it behoved our Saviour to be. Finally, because his death was conjoined with the feeling of the wrath and curse of God, which we by our sins had deserved.

5. Moreover, the promise of the gospel is, that whosoever believeth in Christ crucified, shall not perish, but have everlasting life; which promise ought to be announced and proposed promiscuously and indiscriminately to all nations and men to whom God, in his good pleasure, hath sent the gospel, with the command to repent and believe.

6. But because many who are called by the gospel do not repent, or believe in Christ, but perish in unbelief, this doth not arise from defect or insufficiency of the sacrifice offered by Christ upon the cross, but from their own fault. John iii. 19, 20; v. 44. Heb. iii. 5.

7. But to as many as truly believe, and through the death of Christ are delivered and saved from sin and condemnation, this benefit comes from the sole grace of God, which he owes to no man, given them in Christ from eternity.*

8. For this was the most free counsel, and gracious will and intention of God the Father, that the life giving and saving efficacy of the most precious death of his own Son, should exert itself in all the elect, in order to give

* John i. 12. 1 Cor. xv. 10. Phil. i. 29. 2 Thess. ii. 11—14. "We believe that God (after that the whole race of Adam had been thus precipitated into perdition and destruction by the fault of the first

them alone justifying faith, and thereby to lead them to eternal life: that is, God willed that Christ, through the blood of the cross, (by which he confirmed the new covenant,) should, out of every people, tribe, nation, and language, *efficaciously* redeem all those, and those only, who were from eternity chosen to salvation, and given to him by the Father; that he should confer on them the gift of faith (which, as well as other saving gifts of the Holy Spirit, he obtained by his death); that he should cleanse them by his own blood from all sins, both original and actual, committed after as well as before faith; that he should preserve them faithfully to the end, and at length present them glorious before himself, without any spot and blemish.*

9. This counsel, having proceeded from eternal love to the elect, from the beginning of the world to this present time, the gates of hell in vain striving against it, has been mightily fulfilled, and will henceforth also be fulfilled: so that indeed the elect may in their time be gathered together in one, and that there may always be some church of believers founded in the blood of Christ, who may constantly love the Saviour, who for her, as a bridegroom for his bride, gave up his soul upon the cross, and perseveringly worship and celebrate him here and to all eternity.

---

man,) demonstrated himself to be such as he is in reality, and to have acted as such (*præstitisse*), namely, both merciful and just; MERCIFUL indeed in delivering and saving from damnation and death (*interitu*) those whom, in his eternal counsel, according to his gratuitous goodness by Jesus Christ our Lord, he elected, without any respect to their works; but JUST, in leaving others in that their own fall and perdition into which they had cast themselves headlong." Belgic Confession, Article xvi.

* John vi. 37–40, 44, 65. Eph. v. 25–27. 1 Pet. i. 2–5. Rev. v. 9, 10.

These nine articles are thus *abbreviated* by Tilenus and Heylin.

Art. II. *Of the Merit and Effect of Christ's Death.*

"That Jesus Christ hath not suffered death, but for those elect only; having neither any intent nor commandment from the Father, to make satisfaction for the sins of the whole world." (See Articles iv. v.)

REJECTION OF ERRORS ON THE SECOND CHAPTER.

The orthodox doctrine having been explained, the Synod rejects the errors of those,

1. Who teach "that God the Father destined his own Son unto the death of the cross, without a certain and definite counsel of saving any one by name (*nominatim*), (Rev. xiii. 8; xvii. 8; xx. 15,) so that its own necessity, utility, and meritoriousness (*dignitas*), might be established unimpaired (*sarta tecta*) to the benefit obtained (*impetrationi*) by the death of Christ, and be perfect in its measures (*numeris*), and complete and entire, even if the obtained redemption had not, in fact, been applied to any individual." For this assertion is contumelious to the wisdom of God and the merit of Jesus Christ, and is contrary to Scripture, as the Saviour says, "I lay down my life for the sheep, and I know them." John x. 15, 27. And the prophet Isaiah, concerning the Saviour, "When he shall give himself a sacrifice for sin, he shall see his seed, he shall prolong his days, and the will of JEHOVAH shall prosper in his hand." Isa. liii. 10. And finally, it overturns the article of faith by which we "believe the church."*

* For in this case there might possibly have been no "Church of God, which he hath purchased with his own blood." Acts xx. 28.

2. Who teach "that this was not the end of the death of Christ, that he might, in very deed, confirm the new covenant of grace through his blood; but only that he might acquire a bare right to the Father of entering again into some covenant with men, either of grace or of works." For this contradicts the Scripture, which teaches that "Christ is become the Surety and Mediator of a better covenant." Heb. vii. 22. And a testament is at length ratified in those that are dead. Heb. ix. 15, 17.*

3. Who teach that "Christ, by his satisfaction, did not with certainty (*certo*) merit that very salvation and faith, by which this satisfaction of Christ may be effectually applied unto salvation; but only that he acquired to the Father power, and a plenary will, of acting anew with men, and of prescribing whatever new conditions he willed, the performance of which might depend on the free will of man; and therefore it might so happen either that none or that all might fulfil them." Now these think far too meanly of the death of Christ; they in no wise acknowledge the principal fruit or benefit obtained by it, and recall from hell the Pelagian heresy.†

4. Who teach that "that new covenant of grace, which God the Father, through the intervention of the death of Christ, hath ratified with men, does not consist in this, that by faith, so far as it apprehends the merit of Christ, we are justified before God and saved; but in this, that

---

* Isa. xlii. 6; xlix. 8. Dan. ix. 27. Matt. xxvi. 28. Mark xiv. 24. Gr. Heb. ix. 13—23; xiii. 20.

† That so large a body of learned theologians, collected from various churches, should unanimously, and without hesitation, and in so strong language, declare the error here rejected to be the revival of the Pelagian heresy, may indeed astonish and disgust numbers in

God, having abrogated the exaction of perfect legal obedience, imputes (*reputet*) faith itself, and the imperfect obedience of faith, for the perfect obedience of the law, and graciously reckons it as deserving of the reward of eternal life." For these contradict the Scripture, "They are justified freely by his grace through the redemption made in Jesus Christ, whom God has set forth as a propitiation through faith in his blood." Rom. iii. 24, 25.*

5. Who teach that "all men are taken into a state of reconciliation and the grace of the covenant; so that no one on account of original sin is liable to damnation, or to be damned, but that all are exempt from the condemnation of this sin." For this opinion opposes the Scripture, affirming that "by nature we are the children of wrath."†

6. Who usurp the distinction of impetration and application, that they may instil this opinion into the unwary and inexperienced; that God, as far as pertained to him,

---

our age and land, who oppose something, at least, exceedingly like this against the doctrines called evangelical; but it should lead them to reflect on the subject, and to pray over it. Are they not, in opposing Calvinism, reviving and propagating the heresy of Pelagius?

* "We of good reason and right say with divine Paul, 'That we are justified by faith alone,' or 'by faith without the works of the law.' But, properly speaking, we by no means understand that faith *by itself*, or *of itself*, justifies us; seeing it is that which becomes indeed as an instrument, by which we apprehend Christ our righteousness. Christ therefore himself is our righteousness, who imputes unto us all his own merits, but faith is an instrument by which we are joined to him in the society or communion of all his goods, and are retained in it: insomuch that all these having been made ours, are more than sufficient for us for our absolution from sins." Belgic Confession, Art. xxii.

† See on the third article of the Rejection of Errors, concerning divine Predestination. "Original sin, the fault and corruption of every man that is naturally engendered of the offspring of Adam, in

had willed to confer equally upon all men the benefits which were acquired by the death of Christ; and that some rather than others (*præ aliis*) should be partakers of the remission of sins and eternal life, this discrimination depended on their free will, applying to themselves of the grace indifferently offered, not from an especial gift of mercy operating effectually in them, that they, rather than others, should apply to themselves this grace. For these, while they pretend to propose to themselves this distinction in a wholesome sense, endeavour to give the people a taste of the pernicious poison of Pelagianism.*

---

every person born into this world, deserveth God's wrath and damnation. And although there is no condemnation for them that believe and are baptized, yet the apostle doth confess that concupiscence and lust hath of itself the nature of sin." Art. ix. Church of England.

"We believe that the disobedience of Adam's sin, which they call original (*originis*), hath been spread abroad, and poured out upon the whole human race. But original sin is the corruption of the whole nature, and hereditary vice, by which even infants themselves, in the mother's womb, are polluted; and which, as a certain noxious root, shoots forth (*progerminat*) every kind of sins in man, and is so base and execrable before God, that it suffices for the condemnation of the whole human race. Neither is it to be believed that it is entirely extinguished or pulled up by the roots in baptism; seeing that from it, as from a corrupt fountain, perpetual streams and rivulets continually arise and flow forth, though it does not fall out to condemnation, and is not imputed to the children of God, but is remitted *to them* by the pure grace and mercy of God; not that they should fall asleep confiding in this remission, but that it should excite the more frequent groans (*gemitus*) in the faithful, and that they should more ardently desire to be freed from this body of death. Hence we condemn the error of the Pelagians, who assert that original sin is nothing but imitation." Phil. ii. 13. John xv. 5. Psa. li. 7. Rom. iii. 10. Gen. vi. 3. John iii. 6. Rom. v. 14. Eph. ii. 5. Rom. vii. 18—24. Belgic Confession.

* 1 Cor. xv. 10. Eph. ii. 3—6. Tit. iii. 4—6. Art. x. of the Church of England, on Free-will.

"We believe that the Holy Spirit, dwelling in our hearts, imparts

7. Who teach that "Christ neither could nor ought to die, neither did he die, for those whom God especially (*summe*) loved and chose to eternal life, when to such there was no need of the death of Christ." For they contradict the apostle, saying, "Christ loved me, and gave himself for me." Gal. ii. 20. Also, "Who can lay any thing to the charge of God's elect? It is God that justifieth. Who is he that condemneth? It is Christ who died" (Rom. viii. 32, 34), doubtless for them. And the Saviour who declared, "I lay down my life for my sheep." John x. 15. And, "This is my command, that ye love one another, as I have loved you; greater love hath no man than this, that he lay down his life for his friends." John xv. 12, 13.

CHAPTERS III. & IV.

OF THE DOCTRINE OF MAN'S CORRUPTION, AND OF THE METHOD OF HIS CONVERSION TO GOD.

1. Man, from the beginning, was created in the image of God, adorned in his mind, with the true and saving knowledge of his Creator, and of spiritual things, with righteousness in his will and heart, and purity in all his affections, and thus was altogether holy; but by the instigation of the devil and his own free will (*libera sua voluntate*), revolting from God, he bereaved himself of

---

unto us true faith, that we may attain to the true knowledge of this so great a mystery; which faith embraces Jesus Christ, with all his merits, and claims it to itself, as its proper effect, and seeks thenceforth nothing beyond him." Belgic Confession, Art. xxii.

these inestimable gifts; and, on the contrary, in their place, contracted in himself blindness, horrible darkness, and perversity of judgment in the mind; malice, rebellion, hardness, in the will and heart; and finally, impurity in all his affections.

2. And such as man was after the fall, such children also he begat; namely, being corrupted, corrupt ones, corruption having been derived from Adam to all his posterity, (Christ only excepted,) not by imitation as the Pelagians formerly would have it, but by the propagation of a vicious nature, through the just judgment of God.*

3. Therefore, all men are conceived in sin, and born the children of wrath, indisposed (*inepti*) to all saving good, propense to evil, dead in sins, and the slaves of sin; and without the grace of the regenerating Holy Spirit, they neither are willing nor able to return to God, to correct their depraved nature, or to dispose themselves to the correction of it.†

4. There is indeed remaining in man, since the fall, some light of nature, by the help of which he retains certain notions concerning God and natural things, concerning the difference of things honourable and shameful, and manifests some desire after virtue and external discipline; but so far from his being able by this light of nature to

* "Hence we condemn the error of the Pelagians, who assert that this original sin (*peccatum originis*) is no other thing than imitation." Belgic Confession, Art. xv.

"Original sin standeth not in the following of Adam (*in imitatione Adami,*) as the Pelagians do vainly talk, (*fabulantur*); but it is the fault and corruption of the nature of every man, that naturally is engendered of the offspring of Adam, whereby man is very far gone (*quam longissime distet*) from original righteousness, and is of his own nature inclined to evil, &c. Art. ix. Church of England."

† See on Rejection of Errors, Chap. ii. Art. 6.

attain to the saving knowledge of God, or to turn himself to him, he does not use it rightly in natural and civil things; nay, indeed, whatever thing it may at length be, he contaminates it all in various ways, and holds it in unrighteousness, which when he does he is rendered inexcusable before God.*

5. The reason (or purport or purpose, *ratio*) of the decalogue, particularly delivered from God by Moses to the Jews, is the same as that of the light of nature; for when indeed it exposes the magnitude of sin, and more and more convicts man of guilt, yet it neither discloses a remedy, nor confers the power of emerging from misery; so that, being rendered weak through the transgression of the flesh, it leaves him under the curse, and man cannot through it obtain saving grace.†

6. What, therefore, neither the light of nature nor the law could do, *that* God performs by the power of the Holy Spirit, through the word, or the ministry of reconciliation; which is the Gospel concerning the Messiah, by which it hath pleased God to save believers, as well under the Old as under the New Testament.‡

---

* Man by the fall "entirely withdrew himself from God, (his true life,) and alienated himself, his nature having been wholly vitiated and corrupted by his sin; by which it came to pass, that he rendered himself obnoxious as well to corporeal as to spiritual death. Therefore, having become wicked and perverse, and in all his ways and pursuits (*studiis*) corrupt, he lost all those excellent gifts with which he (God) had adorned him; so that only small sparks and slender remains (*vestigia*) of them are left to him, which yet suffice to render men inexcusable, because whatever there is in us of light hath been turned into blind darkness." Rom. i. 18. 20; ii. 1, 12, 16. Eph. iv. 17—19. Belgic Confession, Art. xiv.

† Rom. iii. 20; v. 20; viii. 3. 2 Cor. iii. 7, 9. Gal. iii. 10, 22.

‡ Rom. viii. 3. Gal. iii. 22. Heb. iv. 1, 2; xi. 7. Both in "the Old

7. God revealed this mystery of his own will to fewer persons under the Old Testament; but now, the distinction of people being taken away, he manifests it to more. The cause of which dispensation is not to be ascribed to the dignity (or worthiness) of one nation above another, or to the better use of the light of nature, but to the most free good pleasure and gratuitous love of God. Therefore they to whom, beyond and contrary to all merit, such grace is given (*fit*), ought to acknowledge it with an humble and thankful heart; in respect of the rest to whom this grace is not given, to adore with the apostle the severity and justice of the judgments of God, but by no means to scrutinize them curiously.†

8. But as many as are invited by the gospel, are invited sincerely (or in earnest, *serio*). For sincerely and most truly God shows in his word what is pleasing to him, namely, that they who are called should come to him. And he sincerely promises to all who come to him and believe, the peace of their souls and eternal life.‡

9. That many who are called by the ministry of the gospel, do not come and are not converted, the fault of this is not in the gospel, nor in Christ offered by the gospel, nor in God inviting by the gospel, and conferring various gifts on them, but in the persons themselves who are invited; some of whom being regardless, (or unconcerned, *securi*,) do not admit the word of eternal life; others indeed admit it (*admittunt*), but do not receive

---

and New Testament, everlasting life is offered to mankind by Christ, who is the only Mediator between God and man, being both God and man."—Art. vii. Church of England.

* See Rejection of Errors on first chapter. Art. ix.

† Matt. xxii. 4—10. John vi. 37—40. Rev. xxi. 6; xxii. 17.

(*immittunt*) it into their heart, so that they turn back after an evanescent joy of temporary faith; and others choke the seed of the word with the thorns of the cares and pleasures of the world, and bring forth no fruit, as our Saviour teaches us in the parable of the sower. Matt. xiii.*

10. And that others, who are called by the ministry of the gospel, do come and are converted, this is not to be ascribed to man, as if distinguishing himself by free-will (*libero arbitrio*) from others, furnished with equal or sufficient grace for faith and conversion, (which the proud heresy of Pelagius states,) but to God, who, as he chose his own people in Christ from eternity, so he also effectually calls them in time, gives them repentance and faith, and, having been rescued (*erutos*) from the power of darkness, translates them into the kingdom of his Son, that they may declare his energies (*virtutes*) who called them out of darkness into this marvellous light, and glory, not in themselves, but in God, the apostolic Scripture everywhere testifying this.†

* Luke vii. 12—15. John iii. 19—21. Heb. iii. 12. iv. 2.

† Whatever things are delivered to us concerning the free-will (*libero arbitrio*) of man, these we deservedly reject, because he is the slave of sin, and man can do nothing of himself, unless it hath been given to him from heaven. For who will dare to boast that he can perform whatsoever things he shall will, when Christ himself saith, "No one can come unto me, except the Father who sent me shall draw him?" Who will boast his own will, who hears that "the affections of the flesh are enmities against God?" Who will glory in his understanding, who knows that the animal man is not capable of those things which are of the Spirit of God? In fine, who will bring forward (*proferat in medium*) any thought of his own, who understands that "we are not sufficient of ourselves to think any thing as of ourselves," but that we are sufficient, all this is of

11. But when God performs his good pleasure in his elect, or works in them true conversion, he not only provides that the gospel should be outwardly preached to them, and that their mind should be powerfully illuminated by the Holy Spirit, that they may rightly understand, and judge what are the things of the Spirit of God; but he also, by the efficacy of the same regenerating Spirit, penetrates into the innermost recesses of man, opens his closed heart, softens his obdurate heart, circumcises his uncircumcised heart, infuses new qualities into his will, makes that which had been dead alive, that which was evil good, that which had been unwilling willing, and from being refractory, obedient; and leads and strengthens it, that as a good tree it may be able to bring forth the fruit of good works.*

12. And this is that regeneration which is so much declared in the Scriptures, a new creation, a resurrection from the dead, a giving of life, (*vivificatio*,) which God *without us*, (that is, without our concurrence) worketh *in us*. And this is by no means effected by the doctrine alone sounding *without*, by moral suasion, or by such a mode of working, that after the operation of God (as far as he is concerned) it should remain in the power of man,

---

God? That which the apostle hath said ought to remain certain and firm: "It is God who worketh in us, both that we may be willing, and that we may effect (*it*) of his own most gratuitous benevolence." Phil. ii. 13. For no mind, no will acquiesces in the will of God, in which Christ himself hath not first worked, which he also teacheth, saying, "Without me ye are able to do nothing." John xv. 5. Belgic Confession, Art. xiv.

* Deut. xxx. 6. Ps. cx. 3, Bible translation. Jer. xxxi. 33; xxxii. 39. Ez. xi. 19; xxxvi. 25, 26. Zech. xii. 10. Matt. xi. 25, 26. John i. 12; iii. 3—6; vi. 44, 45, 65. Eph. ii. 4, 5. Phil. i. 13. Col. i. 13. 1 Thess. ii. 13, 14. Tit. iii. 4—6. 1 Pet. i. 3; ii. 9, 10.

to be regenerated or not regenerated, converted or not converted: but it is manifestly an operation supernatural, at the same time most powerful and most sweet, wonderful, secret, and ineffable in its power, according to the Scripture, (which is inspired by the Author of this operation,) not less than, or inferior to, creation or the resurrection of the dead, so that all those in whose hearts God works in this admirable manner are certainly, infallibly and efficaciously regenerated, and in fact (*actu*) believe.* And thus their will being now renewed, is not only influenced and moved by God, but being acted on by God, itself acts and moves. Wherefore, the man himself, through this grace received, is rightly said to believe and repent.†

13. Believers cannot in this life fully comprehend the manner of this operation; in the meantime they acquiesce in it, because by this grace of God they know and feel that they believe in their heart and love their Saviour.

14. Thus, therefore, faith is the gift of God, not in that it is offered to the will of man by God, but that the thing itself is conferred on him, inspired, infused into him. Not even that God only confers the power of believing, but from thence expects the consent, or the act of believing; but that he, who worketh both to will and to do, worketh in man both to will to believe, and to believe itself (*et velle credere et ipsum credere*), and thus he worketh all things in all.‡

---

* John v. 21, 24, 25. Rom. vi. 4—6; viii. 2. 2 Cor. v. 17, 18. Gal. vi. 15. Eph. i. 19, 20; ii. 6, 10. Col. ii. 12, 13; iii. 1.

† Jer. xxxi. 18, 19. Acts iii. 19; v. 31. Rom. viii. 13. 2 Tim. ii. 25, 26. 1 Pet. i. 22.

‡ "We believe that the Holy Spirit dwelling in our hearts doth impart to us true faith." Belgic Confession, Art. xxii.

15. This grace God owes to no one. For what can he owe to him, who is able to give nothing first, that he may be recompensed? (Rom. xi. 35.) Nay, what can he owe to him, who has nothing of his own but sin and a lie? He, therefore, who receives this grace, owes and renders everlasting thanks to God; he who receives it not, either does not care for those spiritual things, and rests satisfied within himself; or, being secure, he vainly glories that he possesses what he has not. Moreover, concerning those who outwardly profess faith and amend their lives, it is best to judge and speak after the example of the apostles; for the inmost recesses (*penetralia*) of the heart are to us impenetrable. As for those who have not yet been called, it behoves us to pray to God, who calls the things which are not, as though they were; but in no wise are we to act proudly against them (*adversus superbiendum eos est*), as if we had made ourselves to differ. (Rom. xi. 18—20. 1 Cor. iv. 6, 7.)

16. But in like manner, as by the fall man does not cease to be man, endowed with intellect and will, neither has sin, which has pervaded the whole human race, taken away the nature of the human species, but it hath depraved and spiritually stained it; so even this divine grace of regeneration does not act upon men like stocks and trees, nor take away the proprieties (or properties, *proprietates*) of his will, or violently compel it while unwilling; but it spiritually quickens, (or vivifies,) heals, corrects, and sweetly, and at the same time, powerfully inclines it; so that whereas before it was wholly governed by the rebellion and resistance of the flesh, now prompt and sincere obedience of the Spirit may begin to reign, in which the renewal of our spiritual will and our liberty truly consist.

In which manner, (or for which reason,) unless the admirable Author of all good should work in us, there could be no hope to man of rising from the fall, by that *free will*, by which when standing he fell into ruin.*

17. But in the same manner as the omnipotent operation of God, whereby he produces and supports our natural life, doth not exclude, but require the use of means, by which God in his infinite wisdom and goodness sees fit to exercise this his power, so this fore-mentioned supernatural power of God, by which he regenerates us, in no wise excludes or sets aside the use of the gospel, which the most wise God hath ordained as the seed of regeneration and the food of the soul. Wherefore, as the apostles, and those teachers who followed them, have piously instructed the people concerning this grace of God, in order to his glory and to the keeping down of all pride; in the meantime, neither have they neglected (being admonished by the holy gospel) to keep them under the exercise of the word, the sacraments, and discipline: so then be it far from us, that teachers or learners in the church should presume to tempt God, by separating those things, which God, of his own good pleasure, would have most closely united together. For grace is conferred through admonitions, and the more promptly we do our duty, the more illustrious the benefit of God, who worketh in us, is wont to be, and the most rightly doth his work proceed. To whom alone all the glory,

* A more lucid and scriptural exposition of the efficacious influence, by which the regenerating, life-giving, illuminating grace of the Holy Spirit draws, teaches, and inclines the heart to willing and sweet submission and obedience, can hardly be produced from any writer. 2 Cor. x. 5.

both of the means and their beneficial fruits and efficacy, is due för everlasting. Amen.*

These seventeen articles are abbreviated, as above stated, in these two that follow.

Art. III.—*Of Man's Will in a State of Nature.*

"That by Adam's fall his posterity lost their free will, being put to an unavoidable necessity to do, or not to do, whatsoever they do or do not, whether it be good or evil; being thereunto predestinated by the eternal and effectual secret decree of God."

Art. IV. *Of the Manner of Conversion.*

"That God, to save his elect from the corrupt mass, doth beget faith in them, by a power equal to that whereby he created the world and raised up the dead: insomuch, that such unto whom he gives grace cannot reject, and the rest, being reprobate, cannot accept it."†

REJECTION OF ERRORS ON THE THIRD AND FOURTH CHAPTERS.

The orthodox doctrine having been set forth, the Synod rejects the errors of those,

1. Who teach that "it cannot properly be said, that original sin (*peccatum originis,*) suffices of itself for the

* Can any statement be more rational, unexceptionable, and scriptural than this is?

† Let the candid reader compare carefully the seventeen articles above given, with these two abbreviated articles, and then judge for himself, whether such a reporter deserves even the least credit or confidence.

condemnation of the whole human race, or the desert of temporal and eternal punishments;" for they contradict the apostle, who says, (Rom. v. 12), "By one man sin entered into the world, and death by sin; and so death passed upon all men, for that all have sinned." And ver. 16, "By one man the offence entered unto condemnation." Also (Rom. vi. 23), "The wages of sin is death."*

2. Who teach that "spiritual gifts, or good habits and virtues, such as kindness, sanctity, and justice, could have no place in the will of man when he was first created, and therefore neither in the fall could they be separated from it." For this opposes (*pugnat cum*) the description of the image of God, which the apostle states in Eph. iv. 24, where he describes it (as consisting) "in righteousness and holiness," which have a place in the will altogether.

3. Who teach that "spiritual gifts are not separated from the will of man in spiritual death, as it (the will) never was corrupted in itself, but only impeded by the darkness of the mind, and the irregularity of the affections; which impediments being removed, it may be able to exert the free power planted (*insitam*) in it: that is, it might of itself will or choose, or not will or choose, whatever good was proposed to it." This is new and erroneous; even so far as it causes the power of free-will to be exalted, against the words of the prophet, (Jeremiah xvii. 9,) "The heart is deceitful above all things and per-

* "Original sin is so base and execrable, that it suffices to the condemnation of the whole human race." Belgic Confession, Art. xv. "God saw that man had so cast himself into the condemnation of death, both corporeal and spiritual, and was made altogether miserable and accursed." Ibid. Art. xvii. "In every person born into the world, it deserveth God's wrath and damnation." Art. ix. Church of England.

verse :" and the apostle, (Eph. ii. 3,) "Among whom, (contumacious men,) we all had our conversation in times past, in the lusts of our flesh, fulfilling the desires of the flesh and of the thoughts."*

4. Who teach that "man unregenerate is neither properly nor totally dead in sins, or destitute of all power for what is spiritually good; but that he can hunger and thirst after righteousness or life, and offer the sacrifice of a broken and contrite spirit, which is accepted by God." For these things are contrary to the open testimonies of Scripture, (Eph. ii. 14,) "Ye were dead in trespasses and sins." And Gen. vi. 5, and viii. 21, "The imagination of the thoughts of man's heart is only evil continually." Moreover, to hunger and thirst after deliverance from misery, and for life, and to offer unto God the sacrifice of a contrite spirit, is the part of the regenerate, and of those who are said to be blessed. Psa. li. 19. 1 Chron. xxix. 14. Matt. v. 6.

5. Who teach that "man, corrupt, animal, (ψυχικος) can so rightly use common grace, which in them is the light of nature, and the gifts remaining after the fall, that by this good use he may obtain greater grace, for instance, evangelical or saving, and gradually may obtain salvation itself: and on this account God hath showed himself ready, on his part, to reveal Christ to all, seeing that he

* "The apostle says that 'it is God who worketh in us, both that we should will, and that we should do, of his own free benevolence;' for no mind, no will, acquiesces in the will of God, in which Christ himself hath not first operated." Belgic Confession, Art. xiv. "We have no power to do good works, pleasant and acceptable to God, without the grace of God by Christ preventing us, that we may have a good will: and working with us, when we have that good will." Art. x. Church of England.

administers to all, sufficiently and efficaciously, the necessary means to the revelation of Christ, faith and repentance." For, besides the experience of all ages, this is testified to be false by the Scripture, (Psa. cxlvii. 19, 20,) "He showeth his words unto Jacob, his statutes and laws unto Israel; he hath not done so unto any other people, neither have they known his laws." (Acts xvi. 16.) "God permitted in past ages, all the nations to walk in their own ways." Acts xvi. 6, 7. "They were forbidden (Paul and his companions) by the Holy Ghost to preach the word of God in Asia." And "when they were come into Mysia, they endeavored to go towards Bithynia, but the Spirit suffered them not.*

* The matter of fact, that all those who enjoy the means of grace in the greatest abundance, do not profit by them, is as undeniable as that all nations are not favoured with the means of grace; but to speak of those things as *sufficient* and *efficacious*, which in the case of a vast majority prove *insufficient* and *inefficacious*, must surely be unreasonable, especially as to them the Gospel itself proves "a savour of death unto death." That "Paul may plant and Apollos may water," but that God alone can give "the increase," is most manifest to those who have the deepest experience, and have made the most accurate and long-continued observation on the event of the wisest, most loving, and most Scriptural instructions. 1 Cor. iii. 6, 7. Enough has been quoted from the Belgic Confession to show that this error was as contrary to that document, as to any article of the Synod of Dort. "The condition of man after the fall of Adam is such, that he cannot turn or prepare himself, by his own natural strength and good works, to faith and calling upon God." "Works done before the grace of Christ, and the inspiration of his Spirit, are not pleasant to God, forasmuch as they spring not of faith in Jesus Christ; neither do they make men meet to receive grace, or (as the school authors say) deserve grace of congruity; yea, rather, for that they are not done as God hath willed and commanded them to be done, we doubt not but they have the nature of sin." Art. x. xiii. Ch. of Eng. He who is well versed in this controversy, is aware that the doctrine

7. Who teach that "in the true conversion of man there cannot be new qualities, habits, or gifts infused by God into his will; and so faith, by which we are first converted, and from which we are called the faithful, is not a quality or gift infused by God, but only an act of man; nor can it be otherwise called a gift than with respect to the power of attaining it." For these contradict the holy Scriptures, which testify that God doth infuse new qualities of faith, obedience, and a sense of his love into our hearts. Jer. xxxi. 33. "I will put my law into their mind, and will write it in their heart." Isa. xliv. 3. "I will pour water on him that is athirst, and rivers upon the dry ground; I will pour out my Spirit on thy seed." Rom. v. 5. "The love of God which is shed abroad in our hearts by the Holy Spirit which is given to us." They also contradict the constant practice of the church, according to the prophet, praying—"Convert thou me, and I shall be converted." Jer. xxxi. 18, 19. (Ez. xi. 19, 20; xxxvi. 25—27. Eph. i. 19, 20; ii. 8—10.)

7. Who teach "that the grace by which we are converted to God, is nothing else than gentle suasion; or (as others explain it) the most noble method of acting in the conversion of man, and the most suitable (*convenientissimum*) to human nature, is that which is done by suasions, and that nothing hinders that moral grace alone should render animal (*natural*, ψυχικόν) men spiritual; indeed God produces the consent of the will no otherwise than by moral reason; and the efficacy of divine grace, by which he overcomes the operation of Satan, consists in

---

here condemned, comprises the very hinge on which the whole turns; if *false*, Calvinists (in the modern use of the word) are right; if *true*, anti-Calvinists are right.

this, that God promises eternal benefits, and Satan temporal ones." For this is altogether Pelagian, and contrary to the whole Scripture, which, besides this, acknowledges also another and far more effectual and divine mode of acting of the Holy Spirit in man's conversion. Ezek. xxxvi. 26. "I will give you a new heart, and I will put a new spirit within you; and I will take away the heart of stone, and give you a heart of flesh," &c. "Except a man be born again, he cannot see the kingdom of God." John iii. 3—6. "The natural man (ψυχικος) receiveth not the things of the Spirit of God, neither can he know them, because they are spiritually discerned." 1 Cor. ii. 14.

8. Who teach that "God does not apply those powers of his own omnipotence in the regeneration of man, by which he mightily and infallibly bends his will to faith and conversion; but all the operations of grace having been employed (*positis*) which God makes use of in man's conversion, man nevertheless can so resist God and the Spirit, intending his regeneration and willing to regenerate him, and in very deed (*ipso actu*) often doth so resist, as entirely to hinder his own regeneration, and thus it remains in his own power, whether he will be regenerated or not." For this is no other than taking away all the efficacy of God's grace in our conversion, and subjecting the act of Almighty God to the will of man, and contradicts the apostles, who teach that "we believe through the efficacy of the mighty power of God." Eph. i. 19, and that "God fills up in us the good pleasure of his goodness, and the work of faith with power." 2 Thess. i. 11. Also, that "his divine power hath given us all things which pertain to life and godliness." 2 Pet. i. 3. "Thy people shall be willing in the day of thy power." "It is God that worketh in us both to will and to do."

The want of the willing mind is the grand thing wanting, and until this is wrought in us, we "do always resist the Holy Ghost." (Psa. cx. 4. Phil. i. 13.)

9. Who teach that "grace and free will are partial causes concurring at the same time, to the beginning of conversion; nor doth grace, in the order of causality, precede the efficacy of the will; that is, God does not effectually help the will of man to conversion, before the will of man moves and determines itself." For this dogma the ancient church long ago condemned in Pelagius, from the apostle, Rom. ix. 16. "It is not of him that willeth, nor of him that runneth, but of God that showeth mercy." And 1 Cor. iv. 7. "Who maketh thee to differ? And what hast thou that thou didst not receive?" Also, Phil. ii. 13. "It is God who worketh in you this very thing, to will and to do of his good pleasure."*

CHAPTER V.

OF DOCTRINE.

CONCERNING THE PERSEVERANCE OF THE SAINTS.

1. Those whom God, according to his purpose, calleth to the fellowship of his Son, our Lord Jesus Christ, and regenerates by the Holy Spirit, he indeed sets free from the dominion and slavery of sin, but not entirely in this life from the flesh and the body of sin.†

* "Almighty God, we humbly beseech thee that, as by thy *special grace preventing us*, thou dost put into our minds good desires, so, &c." (Collect. East. Sund. Ch. Eng.

† They who constitute the true church; "such a mark of them is the faith by which Christ, or their only Saviour, being apprehended,

2. Hence daily sins of infirmity arise, and blemishes (*nævi*) cleave to the best works even of the saints, which furnish to them continual cause (*materiam*) of humbling themselves before God, of fleeing to Christ crucified, of mortifying the flesh more and more by the spirit of prayer, and the holy exercises of piety, and of panting after the goal of perfection (*ad perfectionis metam suspirandi*) until the time when, delivered from this body of death, they shall reign with the Lamb of God in the heavens.*

3. Because of these remains of indwelling sin, and moreover, also, the temptations of the world and of Satan, the converted could not continue (*perstare*) in this grace, if they were left to their own strength. But God is faithful, who confirms them in the grace once mercifully conferred on them, and powerfully preserves them in the same, even unto the end.†

4. But though that power of God, confirming the truly

they flee from sin and follow after righteousness; at the same time they love the true God and their neighbours, neither turning aside to the right hand nor to the left: they crucify the flesh with its affections, but by no means this indeed, as if there were not in them any longer infirmity: but that they fight against it through the whole time of their life, by the energy (*virtutem*) of the Holy Spirit; and in the mean time they flee to the blood, the death, and the sufferings and obedience of our Lord Christ, as to their most safe protection." Belgic Confession, Art. xxix. Rom. vii. 21—25; viii. 1, 2. Gal. v. 16, 17, 24. See Art. ix. Ch. Eng.—The Remonstrants or Arminians of those days held, it seems, the doctrine of sinless perfection in this life more *generally* than anti-Calvinists do at present.

* "Not that they should slumber, trusting in this remission, but that the feeling of this corruption may excite in the faithful more frequent groans; and that they may wish more ardently to be freed from this body of death. Rom. vii. 18, 24." Belgic Confession, Art. xv.

† Prov. xxviii. 26. Jer. xvii. 9. Luke xxii. 31, 32. 1 Pet. i. 5.

faithful (*vere fideles*) in grace, and preserving them, is greater than what can be overcome by the flesh; yet the converted are not always so influenced and moved by God, that they cannot depart, in certain particular actions, from the leading of grace, and be seduced by the desires (*concupiscentiis*) of the flesh, and obey them. Wherefore, they must continually watch and pray, lest they should be led into temptations. Which, when they do not, they may be not only violently carried away by the flesh, and the world, and Satan, unto grievous and atrocious sins; but they are sometimes even thus violently carried away by the righteous permission of God, which the mournful falls of David and Peter, and of other saints recorded in Scripture, demonstrate.*

5. But by such enormous sins they exceedingly offend God; they incur the guilt of death, they grieve the Holy Spirit, they interrupt the exercise of faith, they most grievously wound conscience, and they sometimes lose, for a time, the perception of grace, until by serious repentance returning into the way, the paternal countenance of God again shines upon them. (Psa. li. 11, 12.)

6. For God, who is rich in mercy, from his immutable purpose of election, does not wholly take away his Holy Spirit from his own, even in lamentable falls; nor does he so permit them to glide down (*prolabi*,) that they should fall from the grace of adoption and the state of justification, or commit the sin unto death, or against the Holy Spirit, that, being deserted by him, they should cast themselves headlong into eternal destruction.†

---

* Psa. cxix. 116, 117. Matt. xxvi. 40, 41, 69–75. 1 Pet. v. 8. Jude 20, 21, 24.

† Luke xxii. 32. John iv. 14. 1 John v. 16–18.

7. In the first place, he preserves in them, in these falls, that immortal seed by which they are regenerated, (*or begotten again, regeniti,*) lest it should perish, or be shaken out. 1 Pet. i. 23. 1 John iii. 9. Then, by his own word and Spirit, he assuredly and efficaciously renews them to repentance, that from the soul they may mourn according to God for the sins committed, may seek remission in the blood of the Mediator by faith, with a contrite heart, and obtain it, that they may feel the favour of God again reconciled, may adore his mercies by faith, and finally, work out their salvation more earnestly with fear and trembling.*

8. So that not by their own merits or strength, but by the gratuitous mercy of God they obtain it, that they neither totally fall from faith and grace, nor finally continue in their falls and perish. Which as to themselves (*quoad ipsos*) not only might easily be done, but would without doubt be done; yet in respect of God, it cannot at all be done, (*or take place, fieri,*) as, neither can his counsel be changed, his promise fall, their vocation according to his purpose be recalled, the merit, intercession, and guardianship of Christ be rendered void, nor the sealing of the Holy Spirit become vain, or be blotted out.†

9. Of this guarding of the elect to salvation, and the perseverance in the faith of the truly faithful, (*vere fidelium,*) the faithful themselves may become certain (*as-*

---

* Can anything be guarded in a more wise, holy, and scriptural manner, than this statement of the means by which God preserves and restores his offending children? Psa. lxxxix. 30—34. Jer. xxxii. 40. 1 Cor. xi. 32. Matt. xxvi. 75. John xxi. 17. 1 Pet. iv. 7; v. 8.

† John x. 27—30; xiii. 36; xiv. 10; xvii. 24. Rom. v. 9, 10; viii. 16, 17, 28—39. 2 Cor. i. 2. Eph. i. 13, 14; v. 30.

sured), and are, according to the measure of their faith, by which they certainly believe themselves to be, and that they shall perpetually remain true and living members of the church, have remission of sins, and eternal life.*

10. And, indeed, (truly *proinde*,) this certainty is not from any peculiar revelation made beyond or without the word of God, but from the belief of the promises which God hath most copiously revealed in his own word for our comfort; by the testimony "of the Holy Spirit witnessing with our spirit, that we are the sons and heirs of God." Rom. viii. 16. Finally, from the earnest (or *serious, serio*) and holy desire (*or pursuit, studio*) of a good conscience and good works.† And of this substantial consolation of the victory to be obtained, and the infallible earnest of eternal glory, if the elect of God could be deprived "in this world, they would of all men be the most miserable."

11. In the mean while, the Scripture testifies that the faithful in this life are assaulted (*conflictari*) with various doubtings of the flesh, and, being placed in heavy temptations, do not always feel this full assurance of faith and certainty of perseverance. But God, "the Father of all consolation," does not suffer them to be tempted above "their strength, but with the temptation makes some way of escape" (*præstat evasionem*, ποιησει εκβασιν) And,

* *May become certain*, not, *are all of them*, or *at all times certain.* Heb. vi. 10, 11. 2 Pet. i. 10, 11. 1 John v. 11—13, 19, 20.

† Surely this has the stamp of holiness deeply impressed upon it! It is evangelical truth, in that part of it, which is most vehemently accused as tending to laxity of practice, and most frequently misstated by the injudicious, and perverted by enthusiasts and hypocrites, set forth in its genuine and inseparable connection with good works. 1 Cor. xv. 58.

by the Holy Spirit, he excites again in the same persons, the certainty of perseverance.

12. But so far is this certainty of perseverance from rendering the truly faithful proud and carnally secure, that, on the contrary, it is the true root of humility, of filial reverential fear, of true piety, of patience in every conflict, of ardent prayers, of constancy in the cross, and in the confession of the truth, and of solid joy in God; and the consideration of this benefit is the spur (*stimulus*) to the serious and continual exercise of gratitude and good works, as it appears by the testimonies of the Scriptures, and the examples of the saints.

13. Neither even in those who are re-instated after a fall, doth the renewed confidence of perseverance produce licentiousness, or neglect (*incuriam*) of piety, but much greater care of solicitously being guarded (or kept) in the ways of God, which are prepared, that by walking in them they may retain the certainty of their own perseverance, lest, on account of the abuse of his paternal benignity, the face of the merciful God, (the contemplation of which is to the pious, sweeter than life, and the withdrawing of it more bitter than death,) should again be turned away from them, and so they should fall into heavier torments of the soul. (Psa. lxxxv. 8.)

14. But as it hath pleased God to begin this work in us by the preaching of the gospel, so by the hearing, reading, meditation of the same, by exhortations, threatenings, promises, and moreover, by the use of the sacraments, he preserves, continues, and perfects it.*

15. This doctrine concerning the perseverance of the

* Is not this a full confutation of those who accuse such as hold this doctrine with rendering all means of grace needless, and all ex-

truly believing and saints, and of its certainty, which God hath abundantly revealed in his word, to the glory of his own name and to the comfort of pious souls, and hath impressed on the hearts of the faithful, the flesh indeed doth not receive, Satan hates, the world derides, the inexperienced (*imperiti*) and hypocrites violently hurry away (*rapiunt*) into abuse, and the spirits of error oppose. But the spouse of Christ hath always most tenderly loved it, as a treasure of inestimable value, and hath constantly defended it (*propugnavit*), which indeed that she may do God will take care (*procurabit*), against whom neither counsel can avail, nor any strength succeed. To whom, the only God, Father, Son, and Holy Spirit, be honour and glory for ever and ever. Amen.

These fifteen articles are abbreviated, as has been above stated, in the following article.

ART. V. *Of the Certainty of Perseverance.*

"That such as have once received that grace by faith, can never fall from it finally or totally, notwithstanding the most enormous sins they can commit."

To which is added, "This is the shortest, and withal the most favourable summary which I have hitherto met with of the conclusions of this Synod, that which was drawn up by the Remonstrants in their *Antidotum*, being much more large, and comprehending many things by

hortations nugatory? The means to be used by the persons themselves, and by others for them, in whatever form they are employed, constitute a part of that counsel and plan, by which God preserves his people, and causes them "to walk religiously in good works, and at length by his mercy they attain to everlasting felicity." Art. xvii. Church of England. Compare Acts xxvii. 22—24, with 31, and Jude 20, 21, with 24.

way of inference which are not positively expressed in the words themselves."

I am not able to annex the *Antidotum* of the Remonstrants: yet I cannot but be disposed to think, that it does not contain a more unfavourable statement of the conclusions made by the Synod of Dort, than that abbreviated in these five articles, though doubtless it is more prolix. But would not the very articles published by the Synod itself, being produced or commented on, have been far more like a *fair* and equitable conduct towards it, than any *abbreviation* or *antidotum*, drawn up by its avowed opponents? I trust such would have been the conduct of most Calvinists, in recording the proceedings of an anti-Calvinistic Synod: but it seems Calvinists are exceptions to all rules, and have no right to expect fair and equitable treatment from other men.

REJECTION OF ERRORS ON THE FIFTH CHAPTER, CONCERNING THE DOCTRINE OF THE PERSEVERANCE OF THE SAINTS.

The orthodox doctrine having been set forth, the Synod rejects the errors of those,

1. Who teach that "the perseverance of the truly faithful is not the effect of election, or the gift of God obtained by the death of Christ, but a condition of the new covenant, to be performed by man, of free-will, antecedent to his *peremptory* election and justification, as they themselves speak." For the sacred Scripture testifies, that it follows election, and that it is given to the elect through the power of the death, resurrection, and intercession of Christ. Rom. xi. 7. "The election have ob-

tained; the rest were hardened." (ἐπωρώθησαν). Also, Rom. viii. 32. "He who spared not his own Son, but delivered him up for us all, how shall he not with him freely give us all things? Who shall lay anything to the charge of God's elect? It is God that justifieth. Who is he that condemneth? It is Christ who died; yea, rather, who is risen again, who also sitteth at the right hand of God, who likewise intercedeth for us. Who shall separate us from the love of Christ?"*

2. Who teach that "God indeed provides the believer with powers sufficient for persevering, and is ready to preserve them in him if he performs his duty: all things, however, being furnished which are necessary to persevering in faith, and which God willeth to supply for the preservation of faith, it always depends upon the freedom of the will whether he will persevere or not persevere:" for this opinion contains manifest Pelagianism; and, while it willeth to make men *free*, makes them sacrilegious, contrary to the perpetual agreement of the evangelical doctrine, which deprives men of all ground (*materiam*) for glorying, and ascribes to divine grace alone the praise of this benefit; and it is opposite to the apostle, who declares that "it is God who will confirm us even to the end blameless, in the day of our Lord Jesus Christ." 1 Cor. i. 8.†

* Luke xxii. 32. 1 Pet. i. 5. "Because the frailty of man without thee cannot but fall; keep us ever by thy help from all things hurtful." Collect, xv. after Trinity, Church of England.

† "Being confident of this, that he who hath begun a good work in you, will perform it until the day of Jesus Christ." Phil. i. 6. If it depend absolutely on the freedom of man's will, whether he will persevere or not, his reliance must and ought to be placed on that, on which the whole event depends; and is not this to trust our own hearts?

3. Who teach that "true believers and regenerate persons may not only fall from justifying faith, and in like manner from grace and salvation, totally and finally, but likewise that in fact (*re ipsa*) they not seldom do fall from it, and perish eternally." For this opinion renders vain the grace itself of justification and regeneration, and the perpetual guardian care (*custodiam*) of Christ, contrary to the express words of the apostle Paul. Rom. v. 8, 9. "If Christ died for us while we were yet sinners, much more, therefore, being now justified through his blood, we shall be saved from wrath by him." And, contrary to the apostle John, (1 John iii. 9,) "Every one that is born of God doth not commit sin, because his seed remaineth in him; neither can he sin, because he is born of God." Also, contrary to the words of Jesus Christ, (John x. 28, 29,) "I give eternal life to my sheep, and they shall never perish, neither shall any one tear them violently out of my hand; my Father who gave them me is greater than all, neither can any one tear them violently out of my Father's hand."

4. Who teach that "true believers and the regenerate may sin the sin unto death, or against the Holy Spirit." But the same apostle, John, chap. v., after, in the 16th and 17th verses, he has mentioned those who sin unto death, and forbidden to pray for them, immediately, ver. 18, adds, "We know, that whosoever is born of God, sinneth not," (namely, in that kind of sin) "but he that is born of God, keepeth himself, and that wicked one toucheth him not."

5. Who teach that "no certainty of future perseverance can be had in this life without special revelation." For by this doctrine solid consolation is taken away from

true believers in this life, and the doubting of the papists (*pontificiorum*) brought back into the church. But the holy Scripture every where requires this certainty, not from special and extraordinary revelation, but from the peculiar marks of the children of God, and the most constant promises of God. In the first place, the apostle Paul, (Rom. viii. 39,) "No created thing can separate us from the love of God, which is in Christ Jesus our Lord," and 1 John iii. 24, "Whoso keepeth his commandment remaineth in him, and he in him; and hereby we know that we remain in him by the Spirit which he hath given us."*

6. Who teach that "the doctrine of perseverance and the assurance of salvation, from its nature and tendency (*indole*), is a pillow for the flesh, and injurious to piety, good conduct, prayers, and other holy exercises; but that on the contrary, to doubt concerning it is laudable." For these persons show themselves to be ignorant of the efficacy of divine grace, and of the operation of the indwelling Holy Spirit; and they contradict the apostle John, affirming in express words, (1 John iii. 2, 3,) "Beloved, now are we the sons of God, but it doth not yet appear what we shall be; we know, however, that when he shall be revealed, we shall be like him, because we shall see him as he is. And whoso hath this hope in him, purifieth him-

---

* 1 John ii. 3, 4; iii. 14, 18, 19. Not a single instance can be adduced from the Scripture, in which any prophet or apostle ascribes his own assurance of salvation to special revelation, or to any thing different from what he exhorts others to, in order to obtain and retain the same assurance. This concludes at least as strongly against those who ground their assurance on dreams, visions, and impressions of whatever kind, as those who say it can only be enjoyed by immediate revelation.

self, even as he is pure." They are, moreover, confuted by the examples of the saints in the Old as well as in the New Testament, who, though they were certain of their own perseverance and salvation, were nevertheless assiduous in prayers and other pious exercises.

7. Who teach that "the faith of temporary believers doth not differ from justifying and saving faith, except in duration alone." For Christ himself, (Matt. xiii. 20, and Luke viii. 13, &c.,) besides this, manifestly constituted a threefold distinction between temporary and true believers, as he says, *those* received the seed in stony ground, *these* in good ground, or "an honest heart;" *those* are without root; *these* have a firm root; *those* are destitute of fruit; *these* bring forth their fruit in divers measures, constantly or perseveringly.*

8. Who teach that "it is not absurd, that the first regeneration being extinct, man should be again, yea, more often regenerated."† For by this doctrine they deny the incorruptibility of the seed of God, by which we are born again, contrary to the testimony of the apostle, 1 Pet. i. 23: "Being born again, not of corruptible seed, but of incorruptible."

9. Who teach that "Christ doth in no wise pray for the infallible perseverance in faith of believers." For they contradict Christ himself, who says, (Luke xxii. 32,) "I have prayed for thee, (Peter,) that thy faith fail not,"

---

* "The foolish virgins took their lamps, but *no oil* with them. The wise took *oil* in their vessels, with their lamps." Matt. xxv. 4, 5. 1 John ii. 19.

† This is a ground that modern opposers of the doctrine not only disclaim, but charge it erroneously as an error which the Calvinists maintain.

and John the evangelist, testifying, (John xvii. 20,) that Christ prayed, not only for the apostles, but likewise for all who shall believe through their words; ver. 11, "Holy Father, keep them through thy name;" and ver. 15, "I pray not that thou mayest take them out of the world, but that thou shouldest keep them from evil."

CONCLUSION.

And this is a perspicuous, simple, and ingenuous declaration of the orthodox doctrine concerning the five controverted articles in Belgium, and a rejection of the errors by which the Belgic churches have for some time been disturbed, which the Synod, having taken from the word of God, judges to be agreeable to the confessions of the Reformed churches. Whence it clearly appears that they, whom it by no means became, purposed to inculcate on the people those (articles) which are contrary to all truth, equity, and charity.

(Namely,) "That the doctrine of the Reformed churches concerning predestination, and the heads connected with it, (*annexis ei*,) by its own proper nature (*genio*) and impulse, draws away the minds of men from all piety and religion;* that it is the pillow of the flesh and of the

* Two things clearly appear from this passage, 1. The Remonstrants assumed it as undoubted that the predestination which they opposed, with its connected heads of doctrine, was generally held by the Reformed churches, including the Church of England. And, 2. They injuriously charged it with involving those very consequences which they who contend that the Church of England is not Calvinistic charge on the doctrine of those whom they call Calvinists.

devil, the citadel of Satan, from which he lies in ambush (*insidietur*) for all, wounds very many, and fatally pierces through many, as well with javelins of desperation as of security. That the same doctrine makes God the author of sin, unjust, a tyrant, a hypocrite; nor is it any other than interpolated Stoicism, Manicheism, Libertinism, and Turcism, (*Turcismum.*)* That it renders men secure, as being persuaded that it does not hinder the salvation of the elect, in what manner soever they live; and they can with safety perpetrate the most atrocious crimes. That it does not profit the reprobate, as to salvation, if they should truly do all the works of the saints. That by the same (doctrine) it is taught that God, by the bare and mere determination (*nudo puroque arbitrio*) of his will, without any respect (views *intuitu*) of the sin of any man, predestinated and created the greatest part of the world to eternal damnation. That in the same manner as election is the fountain and cause of faith and good works, reprobation is the cause of infidelity and impiety. That many unoffending (*innoxiæ*) infants of believers are violently torn away from the breasts of their mothers, and tyranni-

* The chapter in the "Refutation of Calvinism," showing "that the earliest heretics maintained opinions greatly resembling the peculiar tenets of Calvinism," comes far short, it seems, of the charges brought by the Remonstrants against the doctrine of predestination as held by the Reformed churches, including that of England among the rest. That doctrine, as held in these churches, was not only Manicheism, but heathen Stoicism, infidel Libertinism, and Mohammedism. But it is far more easy to bring accusations against any tenet or body of men, than satisfactorily to prove them. The Synod of Dort did not at all shrink from proclaiming that such charges had been brought; and they were satisfied, and on good ground, that they had fully demonstrated them to be unfounded.

cally precipitated into hell; so that neither baptism, nor the prayers of the church at their baptism, profit them."*

Also, those very many other things that are of the same kind, which the Reformed churches not only do not acknowledge, but which they detest with their whole soul (*pectore*). Wherefore, this Synod of Dordrecht, obtests by the name of the Lord, all as many as piously call on the name of our Saviour Jesus Christ, that they would judge concerning the faith of the Reformed churches, not from the calumnies heaped together from this and the other quarter (*hinc inde*), nor even from the private sayings of certain individuals, as well ancient as modern doctors, quoted often either unfaithfully, or wrested (*detortis*) into a foreign meaning; but from the public confessions of those churches and from this declaration of the orthodox doctrine, confirmed by the unanimous consent of all, and every one, of the members of this whole Synod. It then (*deinde*) seriously admonishes the calumniators themselves to consider how heavy a judgment of God they may be about to suffer, who, against so many churches, against so many confessions of churches, bear false witness, disturb the consciences of the weak, and diligently employ themselves (*satagunt*) to render the society of true believers suspected.†

Lastly, this Synod exhorts all their fellow ministers in

---

* The language of these accusations is so horridly irreverend, that if it had not been actually used by the Remonstrants, it could hardly have been thus brought forward; and nothing but to show the real spirit of these controversialists, could excuse the repeating of it, either by the Synod, or in this publication.

† This solemn warning is quite as seasonable in Britain at present as it was in Belgium in the seventeenth century.

the gospel of Christ, that in the treating (*pertractatione*) of this doctrine, they would walk piously and religiously in the schools and in the churches, and apply it, whether by tongue or pen, to the glory of the divine name, to holiness of life, and to the consolation of alarmed souls, that they may not only think, but speak, with the Scripture, according to the analogy of faith; finally, that they would abstain from all those phrases which exceed the prescribed limits of the genuine sense of the Holy Scriptures, and that might afford a just handle to perverse sophists of reviling, or even calumniating the Reformed churches. May Jesus Christ, the Son of God, who, sitting at the right hand of the Father, bestows gifts on men, sanctify us in truth, lead those to the truth who err, shut the mouths of those who calumniate the holy doctrine, and endow the faithful ministers of his word with a spirit of wisdom and discretion, that all their eloquence may tend to the glory of God, and the edification of the hearers. Amen.*

THE DECISION OF THE SYNOD CONCERNING THE REMONSTRANTS.

The truth having been, by the grace of God, thus far explained and asserted, errors rejected and condemned, and iniquitous calumnies refuted, this Synod of Dort, (according to the duty which is further incumbent upon

* Can any thing be more wise, pious, and scriptural, than this concluding counsel and prayer? Who can deny that many called Calvinists, by neglecting the counsel here exhibited, have given much *occasion* of misapprehension, prejudice, and slander to opposers, which might have been avoided? Who can object to this counsel? What pious mind will refuse to add his hearty amen to the closing prayer?

it) seriously, earnestly, and by the authority, which, according to the word of God, it possesses over all the members of its churches, in the name of Christ, beseeches, exhorts, admonishes, and enjoins all and every one of the pastors of the churches in confederated Belgium; the doctors and rectors of the academies and schools, and the magistrates, and indeed all universally, to whom either the care of souls, or the discipline of youth is committed, that, casting away the five known articles of the Remonstrants which are erroneous, and mere hiding places of errors, they will preserve this wholesome doctrine of saving truth, drawn from the most pure fountain of the divine word, sincere and inviolate, according to their ability and office, propound and explain it faithfully to the people and youth, and diligently declare its most sweet and beneficial use in life, as well as in death; that they instruct those of different sentiments, those who wander from the flock, and are led away by the novelty of opinions, meekly by the evidence of the truth, "if peradventure, God will give them repentance to the acknowledgment of the truth; that, restored to a sound mind, they may with one spirit, one mouth, one faith and charity, return to the church of God and the communion of the saints: and that at length the wound of the church may be closed, and all her members be of one heart and mind in the Lord.

But moreover, because some persons, having gone out from among us, under the title of Remonstrants, (which name of Remonstrants, as also of Contra-Remonstrants, the Synod thinks should be blotted out by a perpetual oblivion,) and the discipline and order of the church having been violated, by their endeavours and private counsels in unlawful ways, and the admonitions and judgments of their brethren having been despised, they have grievously, and altogether dangerously disturbed the Belgic churches, before most flourishing, and most united in faith and love, and in these heads of doctrine; have recalled ancient and pernicious errors, and framed new ones, and publicly and privately, both by word and by writings, have scattered them among the common people, and have most vehemently contended for them; have made neither measure nor end of inveighing against the doctrine hitherto received in the churches, by enormous calumnies and reproaches; have filled all things every where, with scandals, dissensions, scruples of consciences, and inventions (*excogitationibus,*) which great crimes certainly against faith, against love, and good morals, and the unity and peace of the churches, as they could not justly be endured in any man, ought necessarily to be animadverted on in pastors, with that most severe censure, which hath in every age (*ab omni œvo*) been adopted by the church, the Synod having invoked the holy name of God, and honestly conscious of its authority from the word of God, treading in the footsteps as well of ancient as of recent Synods, and fortified by the authority of the States General, declares and judges, that those pastors, who have yielded themselves leaders of parties in the church, and teachers of errors, and of a corrupt religion, and of the rended unity of the church, and of most grievous scandals, and moreover, having been summoned before this Synod, of intolerable obstinacy against the decrees of the supreme authority made known by this Synod, and also against the venerable Synod itself, be accounted convicted and guilty persons.

For which causes, in the first place, the Synod interdicts the before cited persons from every ecclesiastical service, and deposes them from their offices, and judges them even to be unworthy of academical functions until by earnest repentance, abundantly proved by words and deeds and contrary exertions, they satisfy the church, and be truly and fully reconciled with the same, and received to her communion; which for their own good and for the joy of the whole church, we peculiarly (*unice*) desire in Christ, our Lord. But the rest, of whom the knowledge hath not come to this national Synod, the Synod commits to the Provincials, the Classes, and the Consistories, after the received order, that they may take care that the church at present receive no detriment, nor fear it hereafter. Let them discriminate with the spirit of prudence the followers of these errors; let them depose the refractory, the clamorous, the factious, the disturbers, as soon as possible from ecclesiastical offices, and those of the schools which belong to their knowledge and care; and let them be admonished that without any interposed delay, after the reception of the decision of this national Synod, having obtained the authority of the magistrate in order to it, they assemble (for this purpose) lest the evil should increase and be strengthened by delay. Let them, with all lenity, by the duties of love, by patience, excite those who have fallen or been carried away by infirmity and the fault of the times, and perhaps hesitate in lighter matters, or are even dissentient, but quiet, of blameless life, tractable, to true and perfect concord with the church; yet so that they may diligently take care that they do not admit any to the sacred ministry who refuse to subscribe these synodical constitutions of the declared doctrine, and to teach it; that they even retain no one, by whose manifest dissension the doctrine approved with such agreement in this Synod may be violated, and the tranquillity of the churches again disturbed.

Moreover, this venerable Synod seriously admonishes all ecclesiastical assemblies, most diligently to watch over the flocks committed to them, and maturely to go and meet all innovations privily springing up in the church, and pull them up, as it were tares, out of the field of the Lord; that they attend to the schools and the conductors (*moderatoribus*) of schools, lest any things, from private sentiments and depraved opinions, having been instilled into the youth, destruction should afterwards be produced to the church and the republic.

Finally, thanks having been reverently given to the States General of Belgium, because they in so necessary and seasonable a time clemently gave succour to the afflicted and declining interests of the church by the remedy of the Synod, that they received the upright and faithful servants of God under their protection, and willed that the pledge of every blessing and the divine presence, the truth of his word, should be in a holy and religious manner preserved in their dominions, that they spared no labour or expense to promote and complete such a work, for which extraordinary benefits the Synod, with its whole heart, prays for the most abundant recompense on them from the Lord, both publicly and privately, both spiritual and temporal. And the Synod indeed most strenuously and humbly asketh the same most clement lords, to will and command that this salutary doctrine, most faithfully expressed according to the word of God, and the consent of the Reformed churches, be alone and publicly heard in these regions; to drive away all heresies and errors privily springing up, and repress unquiet and turbulent spirits, that they would go to approve themselves the true and benign nursing fathers and tutors of the church; that they would determine that the sentence, according to the ecclesiastical authority confirmed by the laws of the country, be valid against the persons before spoken of; and that they would render the Synodical constitutions immovable and perpetual by the addition of their own decision (*calculo*).

On this conclusion a few remarks may be useful.

Conceding that there were things unjustifiable in the decisions made and the measures adopted by the Synod, I would inquire whether all the blame in the whole of that lamentable contest was on one side? Whether the conduct of the Remonstrants was not as remote at least from a conciliatory spirit, as the members of the Synod? And whether, in case the Remonstrants had been victorious, they would have made a more Christian use of their victory and authority than the Synod did? I never yet knew or read of an eager and pertinacious contest, in which both parties were not greatly culpable; and in many instances it is not easy for an impartial observer to determine on which side the greatest degree of criminality rests, only where other motives or prejudices do not counteract, the suffering party is generally favoured and excused, and still more, when the motives, sentiments, or prejudices of the persons concerned are on his side. The Remonstrants, and all who ever since have favoured them, throw the whole blame of the contest, both of the management, result, and consequences of it on the Synod; and as the Remonstrants were, in the first instance, at least, the chief sufferers, and as their tenets are generally more favoured than those of the Synod, the public mind has greatly favoured the cause of the suffering party. Yet the Synod and its supporters seem very confident that the Remonstrants exclusively were in fault, and consider their conduct as intolerably haughty and pertinacious. But will not an impartial judge, would not one who had no sympathy with either party, no partiality or prejudice as to the five points of doctrine, on either side, (if such a man can be found on earth,) would he not fairly divide the criminality? At least would he not allot nearly one half of it to the one, and one half to the other? Nay, might he not allot the greater part to the Remonstrants? Thus, in all other contests which have terminated in incurable separations, the charge of schism has been brought with the utmost confidenee (if not bitterness) by each party against its opponent; and, except in one solitary instance, nearly with equal justice. I say, one instance excepted; for beyond all doubt, on the broad ground of Scripture, in the separation of Protestants from the Roman church, all the guilt of schism rested with that corrupt body which excluded from its communion all those who would not worship creatures, or conform to anti-christian observances; and in many ways made it the duty, the absolute duty of all the true worshippers of God through Christ Jesus, to come forth and be separate. But perhaps this is the only exception.

I would by no means exclude schism from the vocabulary of sins, of great and grievous sins, as many seem disposed to do. Pride, ambition, obstinacy, and self-will, and other very corrupt passions, powerfully influence both those who by spiritual tyranny, would lord it over other men's consciences, and impose things not *scriptural,* if not directly *anti-scriptural,* as terms of communion, or even of exemption from pains and penalties; and also on those who on slight grounds refuse compliance where the requirement is not evidently wrong, and then magnify by a perverse ingenuity, into a most grievous evil, some harmless posture, or garb, or ceremony. If the one party would humbly and meekly, without desiring to arrogate a power not belonging to man, desist from peremptorily requiring such things as are doubtful, and liable to be misunderstood, and so scrupled by upright, peaceable, and conscientious persons; and if the other party would determine to comply, as far as on much previous examination of the Scripture, with prayer and teachableness, they conscientiously could do it, the schism might be prevented, and all the very bad effects of the church of Christ being thus rent and split into parties, prevented. For these several parties are generally more eager in disputing with each other, than "contending for the faith once delivered to the saints;" in making proselytes, than in seeking the conversion of sinners, and in rendering their opponents odious and ridiculous, than in exhibiting our holy religion as lovely and attractive to all around them. In these things, their zeal spends itself to no good purpose.

As to the existing divisions, it appears to me, on long and patient investigation, that they originated from very great criminality on both sides; nor am I prepared to say, on which side it was the greater, and that there is criminality on both sides, in the continuance of them, and still more in the increase of them, in which the heaviest lies, on those who hastily, and on very doubtful or inadequate grounds, make new separations. Yet as to the general division of the Christians in England, into churchmen and dissenters, it appears to me, that in present circumstances, neither individuals, nor public bodies, can do anything to terminate it; nor till some unforeseen event make way for a termination, by means, and in a manner, of which little conception can previously be formed. In the mean while, it seems very desirable to abate acrimony and severity, and to differ, where we must differ, in a loving spirit; and to unite with each other in every good work, as far as we can conscientiously. It is in my view in this case precisely the same as it was with the Synod of Dort and the Remonstrants, each party throws the whole blame on the other; but impartiality would, I think, nearly allot half to the one and half to the other. True Christians of every description live surrounded with ungodly men, nay, such as are profane, and immoral, and contentious, yet they generally are enabled to live peaceably with them all. How is it, then, that they cannot, on the same principles, bear with each other, when differences in merely the circumstances of religion are the only ground of disputations, bickerings, and contests? "Whence come fightings among them?"

2. A large proportion of that which at present would be disapproved, if not reprobated, in the concluding decision of the Synod of Dort, and in its effects, must be considered by every impartial and well informed person as pertaining to that age, and those which had preceded it. The authority of such conventions to determine points of theology, to enforce their decisions by ecclesiastical censures, interdicts, and mandates, such as this conclusion contains, had not been called in question, at least in any great de-

gree, by any of the Reformers or Reformed churches. It was the general opinion, that princes and states ought to convene councils or assemblies when needed, and, as far as hope was given of such councils being convened, they acted on this principle. They considered the ruling powers as invested with the right of authorizing these conventions to cite before them the persons whose tenets and conduct gave occasion of convening them, and of animadverting on them as contumacious, if they refused to appear or to submit to the decisions of the majority. And they regarded it as a great advantage when the secular power would concur in carrying into effect their censures, exclusions, or requirements. These points had been almost unanimously assumed as indisputable from the dawn of the Reformation to the time of this Synod, both on the continent and in Britain; and little had been advanced in direct opposition to the justice of proceeding still further to punish the refractory with pains and penalties. The vanquished party indeed generally complained and remonstrated with sufficient acrimony, yet when the tables were turned, and they acquired a victory, they used their superiority in the same manner, and sometimes even with still greater severity. How far all this was criminal, unscriptural, unreasonable, or not, is by no means the present question, but how far the Synod of Dort went beyond the precedents of former times, and of other countries.

3. Thus far, it seems to me at least, the case is clear, and to an impartial mind not difficult; but how far the whole of this procedure, either in this Synod, or in other similar cases on the continent and in our land, was wrong, *in toto* or *in parte*, whether the whole must be reprobated

together, or only some part of it, or where the line should be drawn, are questions of greater difficulty, on which men in general will decide according to the prevailing sentiments of the day, and those of that part of the visible church to which they belong. Yet I would venture with a kind of trepidation, and with much diffidence, to drop a few hints on the subject, the result of very much reflection during a long course of years, with what other aid I could procure, in addition to the grand standard of truth and duty, of principle and practice, to men of all ranks, individually, or in corporate bodies, the "Oracles of God."

It must, as it appears to me, be incontrovertible, that penal means, of whatever kind, are wholly inadmissible in matters purely religious; and in which the persons concerned would act peaceably, if not irritated by opposition and persecution, for oppression in this case often maketh a wise man mad, and his mad conduct is ascribed to his religious peculiarities, when it originates from other causes, and is excited by oppression. Punishments can have no tendency to enlighten the understanding, inform the mind, or regulate the judgment; and they infallibly increase prejudice and tempt to resentment. They may indeed make hypocrites, but not believers; formalists, but not spiritual worshippers; and, in a word, they are no "means of grace" of God's appointment, and on which his blessing may be expected and supplicated. The weapons of this warfare are carnal, not mighty through God. The judicial law of Moses, as a part of the theocracy, punished with death nothing but idolatry and blasphemy, and this to prevent the contagion; "that men might hear, and fear, and do no more such wickedness," not to produce conviction or conformity; and no penalty in other things was appointed, where the public peace was not interrupted, and God's appointed rulers opposed. In the New Testament not a word occurs on the subject, except as our Lord blamed the apostles when they forbade one to cast out devils because he followed not with them.

Whatever company in any nation can give proper security that they will act as peaceful citizens and good subjects, has, I apprehend, a right to the protection of the state, whatever its religious opinions or observances may be, provided nothing grossly immoral, and contrary to the general laws of the country, be practised under the pretence of religion. Yet the murders, human sacrifices, and other abominations in the East Indies, and in many other places, can have no right to toleration, nor can the toleration be by any means excused. Again, whatever may be urged in favour of allowing Papists full liberty as to their superstitious and idolatrous worship, (for so it doubtless is,) this should be done in their case with peculiar circumspection. But to grant them what they claim, and many claim for them, as *emancipation*, and which means nothing else than *admission to power and authority*, seems irreconcilable to wisdom, either human or divine. It is an essential principle of popery, however disguised by some, and lost sight of by others, *to tolerate none who are not of that church;* and the grant of power to them, till this principle be disavowed by bishops, vicars-general, legates, cardinals, and popes, as well as others, in the most full and unequivocal language, is to liberate lions, because they have been harmless when not at liberty; and the event, should this *emancipation* be fully conceded, will be that the power thus obtained will be used in persecution of those who gave it, as soon as it has acquired a proper measure of consolidation. If the advocates for this measure in our land, should they prove successful, do not themselves live to feel this, their posterity, I can have no doubt, will know it by deplorable experience. Avowed atheists seem also inadmissible to full toleration, as incapable of being bound by any obligation of an oath, or of an affirmation, as in the sight of God, which is equivalent to an oath. How far some kinds of blasphemers should be also exempted may be a question; but every species of profaneness or impiety is not direct blasphemy. Yet if men outrage, or expose to ridicule or odium, the most sacred services of the religion of the country, or if public instructors inculcate immoral principles, they may, as far as I can see, be restrained, so that the mischief may be prevented, though perhaps without further punishment, except for actual violation of the peace. Every collective body, however, has an indisputable right to prescribe the terms on which men shall be admitted into it, either as members of the company, or in an official capacity; and if it have funds at its disposal, the terms on which men shall be allowed to receive a share of them, provided that they who join them do it *voluntarily*, and that others may, without molestation, be permitted to decline these terms, or to withdraw, if they, after having joined them, can no longer conscientiously comply. I say a *right* indisputable by man, yet a *right* for the use of which they are responsible to God, and the abuse of which has been and is the source of most deplorable consequences.

If, however, the Synod of Dort had only proceeded to exclude from *office*, public teachers, whether of congregations or schools, belonging to the church or churches established in Belgium, who would not comply with the terms agreed on in the Synod, the *terms* alone would have been the proper subject of our judgment, and not this *exclusion*, provided no further punishment had been inflicted. But this exclusion (*ex officio*) would of course be also (*ex beneficio*), or from the emolument of the office. And how far this would have been justifiable, I am not prepared to say; and, indeed, much depended on the nature of their funds, and the tenure on which they were obtained or held. But one thing is clear, that if some reasonable proportion of the emolument had been reserved to those who were excluded from office, so long as they conducted themselves peaceably, it would have been a very conciliatory measure, and suited to give a convincing testimony, that the glory of God, the peace of the church, the cause of truth, and the salvation of souls had been their motives and object, and not secular and party interests.

In respect of those revenues which, having been appropriated to religious purposes in former ages, fell into the hands of those who conducted the Reformation and formed establishments, it cannot reasonably be expected that the bodies thus in possession should voluntarily agree to share them with dissentients; but in revenues raised by taxes on the present generation, for the purposes of supporting religion, and other things connected with it, equity seems to require that a proportion should be awarded to peaceful dissentients, of whatever description, according to the sum which that whole body may be required to pay towards such a tax; for they who contribute and are good subjects, and can give a pledge to the government of good behaviour, ought, in all reason, to share the benefit in proportion.*

* It may be worthy of consideration, how far a grant from parlia-

When the teachers of congregations and of schools, supported by the revenues of the churches in Belgium, had been excluded or suspended from their office and its emolument, all that was done in accession, seems to have been unjustifiable. The excluded party, in reason, and according to the Scripture, (though not according to the general sentiments of that age,) were entitled to full toleration, to worship God, and instruct others either as preachers or teachers of schools, not supported by the establishment, provided they did this peaceably. At most, only very general restrictions should have been required. But such teachers of separate congregations, and of schools, were not then known, or at least not recognized; nearly all places of worship and schools were in the hands of the established authorities, and every thing attempted must be done secretly, and then, on that very ground, condemned as a *conventicle* or seditious meeting.

Excommunication, according to Scripture, is nothing more than simple exclusion from the communion of the church: "let him be as an heathen man, and a publican:" except when God *miraculously* by his apostles, who could, in that respect, "do nothing against the truth, but for the truth," inflicted salutary chastisements, "for the destruction of the flesh, that the spirit might be saved in the day of the Lord Jesus;" or that "others might learn not to blaspheme." But when, in addition to such an exclusion,

---

ment for building churches or chapels exclusively for the establishment, while the public at large must advance the money from the general tax or taxes, is thus consistent with strict equity. The design is excellent and most desirable; but whether it would not be more unexceptionable if a proportionable sum were granted to peaceable dissenters, for the building or repairing their places of worship, may be matter of inquiry to impartial legislators.

many heavy consequences followed, even to fines, banishment, imprisonment, exclusion from the common benefits of society, and even death, the very word *excommunication* became dreadful and hateful; and the relaxation of all discipline, nay, almost its annihilation, has been the consequence. Restore the matter to its original use; let the communicants become such of their own *voluntary* choice, admitted on a simple and credible profession of those things in which Christianity consists; and let them, if they act inconsistently, be excluded from communion, and left in their former state till they give proof of repentance; considered as equally entitled to good will and good offices in temporal things, as our other neighbours; admitted to any means of grace which may aid their recovery; conversed with in every way which does not sanction their misconduct; and "restored," if it may be, in "the spirit of meekness." On this plan, I apprehend, discipline might again be established, and great benefit arise from it. But they who cannot inflict miraculous judgments surely are not authorized to attempt other punishments of excommunicated persons, which have a thousand times oftener been exercised against the truth than for the truth.

The distinctions among the different offenders, and the mandates given to the different subordinate classes and presbyteries, appear in no other way exceptionable, than as the Presbyterian plan will of course be objected to, both by Episcopalians and Independents. But the Synod, as it has been seen, attempted far too much; and, forgetful of our Lord's prohibition, were so eager to root up the tares that they greatly endangered the wheat also.

THE APPROBATION OF THE STATES GENERAL.

The States General of federated Belgium, to all who shall see and read this, health (or salvation, *salutem*). We make it known (that) when in order to take away those lamentable and pernicious controversies which, a few years since, with great detriment to the republic and disturbance of the peace of the churches, arose concerning the known five heads of Christian doctrine, and those things which depend on them, it seemed proper to us according to the order in the church of God, and thus also in the Belgic church, to convene at Dordrecht a national Synod of all federated Belgium; and that this might be celebrated (*celebrari*) with the greatest fruit and advantage of the republic, not without much inconvenience (*molestia*) and great expenses, we sought for and obtained unto the same, very many, the most excellent, learned, and celebrated foreign theologians of the Reformed church, as it may be seen from the subscription of the decrees of the aforesaid Synod, after each of the heads of doctrine. Moreover, our delegates being also commissioned (*deputatis*) from each of the provinces, who, from the beginning to the end, being present, should take care that all things might there be handled in the fear of God, and in right order from the word of God alone, in agreement to our sincere intention; and when this aforesaid Synod, by the singular blessing of God, hath now judged with so great a consent of all and every one, as well of foreigners as of Belgians, concerning the aforementioned five heads of doctrine, and the teachers of them; and we, having been consulted, and consenting, published on the sixth of May last past, the decrees and determination affixed to these presents; we, that the much wished for fruits from this great and holy work (such a one as the Reformed churches have never before this time seen) might be abundant to the churches of these countries, seeing that nothing is to us equally desired and cared for as the glory of the most holy name of God, and the preservation and propagation of the true Reformed Christian religion, (which is the foundation of prosperity and bond of union of *federated Belgium*,) as the concord, the tranquillity, and the peace of the churches, and in like manner the preservation of the concord and communion of the churches in these regions with all foreign Reformed churches, from which we never ought, nor are able to separate ourselves; having seen and known, and maturely examined and weighed the aforementioned judgment and decision of the Synod, we have fully in all things approved them, confirmed and ratified them, and by these presents we do approve and ratify them, willing and enacting (*statuentes*) that no other doctrine concerning the aforesaid five heads of doctrine be taught or propagated in the churches of these regions, besides that which is conformable and agreeable to the aforesaid judgment; enjoining and commanding with authority to all the ecclesiastical assemblies, the ministers of the churches, the professors and doctors of sacred theology, the rulers of colleges, and to all in general, and to every one without exception, (*in universum*) whom these things can in any way concern or reach unto, that in the exercise of their ministerial offices and functions, they should in all things follow them faithfully, and sincerely conduct themselves consistently with them. And that this our good intention may every where be fully and in all things satisfied, (or complied with,) we charge and command the orders, governors, the deputies of the orders, the counsellors, and deputed orders of the provinces of Gueldria, and the county of Zutphen, of Holland, West Friesland, Zealand, Utrecht, Frisia, Overyssel, and of the state of Groningen, and the Omlandias, and all their officiaries, judges, and justiciaries, that they should promote and defend the observation of the aforesaid Synodical judgment, and of those things which depend on it, so that they should not either themselves make any change in these things, or permit it by any means to be done by others; because we judge that it ought to be so done to promote the glory of God, the security and safety of the state of these regions, and the tranquillity and peace of the church. Given (*actum*) under our seal, and it hath been sealed by the sealing of the president, and the subscription of our secretary, the count of Hague, the second of July, in the year 1619. A. PLOOS.

As also beneath,

By the mandate of the States General.

Subscribed, C. AERSSEN.

And in that space, the aforesaid seal was impressed on red wax.

On this document, it must be again observed, that the measure adopted by the rulers of Belgium, in respect of the decisions of the Synod of Dort, ought not to be judged according to the generally prevailing sentiments of modern times. An immense revolution in opinion, on these subjects, has taken place, within the last two centuries: and to render these rulers and this Synod amenable to what we may call *statutes long after enacted*, as if whatever there was wrong in the conduct, was *exclusively* their fault, would be palpably unjust. "Are ye not partial in yourselves, and are become judges of evil thoughts?" James ii. 4. "But the wisdom from above is without *partiality.*" James iii. 18. The general *principle* of inducing, by coercive measures, conformity in doctrine and worship, to the decisions of either councils, convocations, synods, or parliaments, was almost universally admitted and acted upon to a later period, than that of this Synod; and though not long afterwards it was questioned, and in some instances relinquished, yet it retained a very general prevalency, for at least half a century after; nor is it without its advocates, even in the Reformed churches, at this present day. Had the opponents of the Synod possessed the same authority, they would have acted in like manner, and so would the rulers of the other countries in Europe. The *exclusive* charge therefore against the measures under consideration, must be laid in those things which were *peculiar* in their proceedings.

As authority and compulsion can never produce conviction, or any regulation of the mind and judgment, the word *sincerely* in this state-paper is very improperly used.

It could not indeed reasonably be expected, that even external conformity to so exact and extensive a doctrinal standard, could be generally or durably accomplished; but to suppose that any thing beyond this would be the result, except what argument and explanation, and appeals to the Scriptures, in the articles of the Synod itself could effect, was evidently most irrational, yet it was the notion of the times, and does not still appear absurd to all men, even in Protestant countries.

Had the rulers of Belgium adopted and ratified the decisions of the Synod, as approving and recommending them to all the persons concerned, and giving countenance in some measure to those who voluntarily avowed the purpose of adhering to them, and leaving others entirely at liberty to decline these terms, whether as authorized teachers of congregations or of schools, but no further molesting them, or interfering with their pursuits or instructions, their conduct might have been advocated, especially if, as it was said before, some fair portion of their former incomes had been reserved to those who relinquished their situations rather than promise to conform, but who otherwise behaved as peaceful members of the community. But by absolute authority to demand of all entire conformity, whether voluntary or involuntary, and to follow up this demand by the secular arm, and by heavy punishments, was altogether unjustifiable. Yet, except the strictness of the rule itself, what country almost was there in Europe at that time, or which almost of either the rulers or teachers of the Reformed churches, that did not in great measure attempt to do the same? So that while authority, in many instances, repeatedly shifted sides, whichever part was uppermost, its religious decisions were enforced by similar measures.

"The Reformers dissented from almost every principle of the church of Rome but this, the right of persecution, and though Luther and some others thought it rather too much to *burn* heretics, all agreed that they should be restrained and punished, and in short, that it was better to burn them than to tolerate them. The church of England has burnt Protestants for heresy, and Papists for treason. The church of Scotland, and the London ministers in the interregnum declared their utter detestation and abhorrence of the evil of *toleration*, patronizing and promoting all other errors, heresies, and blasphemies whatever, under the abused name of liberty of conscience." (*Williams on Religious Liberty, Eclectic Review.*)

The main point in this quotation is indisputable; but in respect of Luther especially, it is erroneous. It would, probably, be difficult to produce an instance in which this great man even so much as sanctioned the punishment of the wild enthusiasts and deceivers of his day, except where the peace of society rendered the interposition of the magistrate indispensable.—"At the same time, he (Luther) took occasion to reprobate the cruel sufferings inflicted on the poor wretches by the persecutions of the ecclesiastical rulers, insisting with the utmost precision on that grand distinction of which this Reformer never lost sight; that errors in articles of faith were not to be suppressed by fire and sword, but confuted by the word of God, and that recourse was never to be had to capital penalties, except in cases of actual sedition and tumult." (Milner's Eccl. Hist. vol. iv. p. 1098.)

"His worthy friend Lineus, probably in a state of irritation, had asked him whether he conceived a magistrate to be justified in putting to death teachers of false religion—a question then little understood, and not generally agreed upon till long afterwards. I am backward, replied Luther, to pass a sentence of death, let the demerit be ever so apparent; for I am alarmed when I reflect on the conduct of the Papists, who have so often abused the statutes of capital punishments, against heresy, to the effusion of innocent blood. Among the Protestants, in process of time, I foresee a great probability of a similar abuse, if they should now arm the magistrate with the same powers, and there should be left on record a single instance of a person having suffered legally for the propagation of false doctrine. On this ground, I am decidedly against capital punishment in such cases, and think it *quite sufficient* that mischievous teachers of religion be removed from their situations." (Milner's Eccl. Hist. vol. v. p. 1100.)

But whatever were the opinions or practice of those times in this respect, or whatever the sentiments of any in our times may be, it seems to me incontrovertible, that every church or associated company of Christians, whether as a national establishment, or in any other form, has a right (for the use of which they are responsible to God alone) to appoint the terms on which such as *voluntarily* desire it, shall be admitted to communion with them, or to teach as pastors and as tutors in their schools and academies, to refuse admission to such as do not agree to these terms, and to exclude those who afterwards act contrary to them. And if they have funds, which are probably *their own*, they have a right to employ these funds to the exclusive support of such as voluntarily concur with them, *volenti non fit injuria;* and it is absurd to deem those *compelled*, or their liberty infringed, who *of their own voluntary will* choose to conform, whether under an establishment or elsewhere. The Eclectic Review on "Gisborne on the Colossians," says, "Was it possible for the author of these discourses to put down a sentiment so just and so weighty as this, without the perception of its censure bearing against the rites and ceremonies of his own church? Is there nothing of will-worship in that communion? What are sponsors, and the sign of the cross in baptism, the *compulsion* to kneel at the Lord's supper, but new commands and prohibitions added to those which are established in the Bible?—(Eclectic Review, May 1817, p. 481).

My concern at present is only with the word *compulsion*. Can it be conceived, that they who voluntarily come to the Lord's Supper in the Church of England, consider *kneeling* as *compulsion?* And who is at present *compelled* to receive the Lord's Supper in that church? Some indeed are *tempted*, too strongly tempted, but none are *compelled*. Again, would it not excite at least as much surprise and perplexity in a dissenting congregation, both to minister and communicants, if one or more of the company should kneel down to receive the bread and wine, and refuse to receive them in any other posture, as it would in a church, if one or more should sit down, or stand, or refuse to kneel at the time of receiving? Should the custom of receiving in a sitting posture be considered as *compulsion*, and as a command or prohibition added to those which are established in the Bible? By no means. Each company has its usage, whether established by law, or by the appointment of an independent church. That usage is known; it is seldom seen that a communicant expresses the least objection to it. He is *voluntary*, or he need not come. Whether kneeling as uniting solemn prayer with receiving, or sitting, as among Presbyterians and Independents, or standing, or reclining on couches, (the posture no doubt of the apostles, at its institution,) if it be *voluntary* in each person, there is no infringement of *liberty*, whatever else may be controverted, respecting the posture.

But to return to Belgium and the Synod of Dort. There toleration of dissentients was not thought of; and the effort was made to enforce conformity on the whole mass of the population, especially on public teachers, and this, not only by exclusions, but by very severe disqualifications and other punishments. And probably the change of sentiment and practice in Belgium in this particular, which soon afterwards took place, and the toleration granted there, before it had any legal ground in Britain, combined in augmenting the general odium against the measures connected with this Synod.

However, I do, in may private judgment, consider the articles of the Synod of Dort as very *scriptural*, yet, when made the terms of conformity, or of officiating as public teachers, even with full toleration and exemption from any thing beyond simple exclusion, I must regard them as peculiarly *improper*. The terms of communion, even where none are molested who decline them, and of being public teachers, should by no means be carried into all the *minutiæ* of doctrine, which perhaps the ablest theologians are convinced to be scriptural. They should include only the grand principles in which all the humble disciples and pious ministers of Christ agree, and not those in which they are left to differ. "Him that is weak in the faith, receive ye, but not to doubtful disputations."

The apostles never attempted to enforce by authority, the whole of what they *infallibly knew* to be true. And who then should attempt to enforce their *fallible* opinions on others? Besides, by aiming at too much, the very end is defeated: the numbers who, from ignorance or indolence, and corrupt motives, conform in such cases, and of those who teach other doctrines than what they have consented to, becomes too great for any discipline to be exercised over them. Many, also, of the most pious and laborious teachers who, in one way or other, manage to explain the established articles in their own favour, or at least as not against them, add greatly to the difficulty and evil: and so all discipline is neglected, as facts deplorably prove.

Probably, this has been, and is in a measure, the case, in most or all of the churches; but the proceedings of the Synod of Dort, and of the rulers of Belgium at that season, were more exceptionable than those of any other, at least as far as I can judge. And this appears to me the chief blame to which they are justly exposed; but which is almost, if not wholly, overlooked, in the torrent of indiscriminate invective in which they, and these transactions, have been long overwhelmed.

THE END.

www.ingramcontent.com/pod-product-compliance
Lightning Source LLC
LaVergne TN
LVHW010246110826
845151LV00004B/1406

* 9 7 8 1 4 2 5 5 2 3 4 4 2 *